THE EPISTLE TO TITUS
and
THE EPISTLE TO PHILEMON

NEW TESTAMENT FOR SPIRITUAL READING

VOLUME 20

Edited by

John L. McKenzie, S.J.

THE EPISTLE
TO TITUS

JOSEF REUSS

THE EPISTLE
TO PHILEMON

ALOIS STÖGER

CROSSROAD · NEW YORK

2587

1981
The Crossroad Publishing Company
575 Lexington Avenue, New York, NY 10022

Originally published as *Der Brief an Titus*
and *Der Brief an Philemon*
© 1966, 1965 by Patmos-Verlag
from the series *Geistliche Schriftlesung*
edited by Wolfgang Trilling
with Karl Hermann Schelke and Heinz Schürmann

English translation © 1971 by Sheed and Ward, Ltd.
Translated by Michael Dunne

Library of Congress Catalog Card Number: 81-68177
ISBN: 0-8245-0129-2

PREFACE

The epistle to Titus with the two epistles to Timothy are called pastoral epistles. Unlike the epistles which precede them, they are addressed not to an entire church but to a single officer; apart from these pastoral epistles Paul mentions neither the official titles nor the names of the persons to whom the epistles were delivered. Josef Reuss suggests that the letter to Titus was addressed to the whole church and not merely to its chief officer. We know nothing of the office and function which Titus exercised in Crete outside of what the epistle tells us. There is no parallel to the position of Titus; he was not an apostle, neither was he a bishop as the office developed later. He was the personal representative of Paul; in the apostolic church a precise delegation of responsibility was not necessary.

This is one of the epistles which are commonly attributed to the school of Paul or the tradition of Paul. The epistle exhibits a concern with church order and with doctrine which is not found in the earlier epistles, those which are attributed to Paul without doubt. It is thought that this reflects a more developed ecclesial polity than the churches of the first generation possessed. The authority of the church officer is more clearly asserted; the officer is more of a teacher than an apostle. The impression is given that he exercises closer supervision over the moral conduct of the members of the church than the early epistles of Paul exhibit.

Nevertheless, the centrality of Christ in the church is still apparent. The epistle speaks of two "appearances" of grace and glory. The first is in the life of Jesus Christ (2:11; 3:4) which introduces salvation; the second (2:13) is the eschatological coming of the Lord which will bring salvation to fullness. The church lives between these two appearances.

The epistle to Philemon, while it is addressed to Philemon and others, is the nearest to a personal letter of all the epistles of Paul. It deals directly with a social problem touched more than once in the New Testament, the problem of slavery. Modern readers sometimes wonder why the New Testament writings do not suggest a social revolution which would overturn slavery; they find the New Testament acceptance of slavery an intolerable compromise. Revolution is not the gospel way of attacking social problems; the gospel aims realistically at the change of the minds of the men who make up society, and not merely at the change of laws and institutions. Roman law prescribed the return of fugitive slaves to their owners. Paul returns the fugitive slave Onesimus with the request that Philemon receive him as a brother. There precisely is the Christian revolution, that slaves and owners are brothers. A Christian slaveholding system is impossible, but it is meaningless to say this until brotherhood is perceived. Paul reminds Philemon that he is eternally obligated to Paul for his faith, which Paul elsewhere describes as freedom in Christ Jesus. It is up to Philemon to see how Onesimus enjoys the same freedom in Christ Jesus which both he and Onesimus received in baptism. We who do not live in slave-owning society can hardly grasp the revolutionary character of Paul's request—not a command—that Philemon accept his slave as a brother; but our society still finds the belief that all men are brothers too revolutionary for its taste.

JOHN L. McKENZIE.

The Epistle to Titus

INTRODUCTION

Teach What Befits Sound Doctrine

The Epistle to Titus is, with the First and Second Epistle to Timothy, one of the group of pastoral epistles. These letters are very similar to each other in form and content and so constitute a special group of Paul's letters. All three of them are addressed to individuals, to the Apostle's fellow workers, but they are at the same time official writings addressed to the communities headed by their pastors, Timothy and Titus. All three letters deal with the duties of the pastoral ministry, and contain similar directives and instructions. All three presuppose the same historical situation, and have language, vocabulary, and spirit in common.

These " pastoral letters " come from the last period in St. Paul's life. It is likely that, after having been set free in 63 AD from his first Roman captivity, the Apostle attempted a missionary journey in Spain, but we have no definite information about this. He then returned to Asia Minor and Greece, and also visited the island of Crete, where, with Titus, he established some Christian communities (1:5).

Titus' parents were pagan (Gal. 2:3), and he was probably converted to Christianity by Paul himself (1:4); he was a member of the Christian church at Antioch. Without having been circumcised, he traveled with Paul and Barnabas to the Apostles' Council in Jerusalem (Gal. 2:1-5). Apart from that we do not know on what journeys he accompanied Paul, since, strangely enough, the Acts of the Apostles tells us nothing about him. Towards the end of the third missionary journey, he was sent from Ephesus to Corinth with the letter "written with many tears." The Corinthian community was almost lost to the Apostle, but through his skill in discharging his mission he won them back. Soon afterwards, Paul sent him again from Macedonia to Corinth, to complete the collection of money there, and at the same time to deliver the Second Epistle to the Corinthians (2 Cor. 6:16–23; 12:18). After working together in Crete, Paul left him behind (1:5) to continue the missionary activity, and especially to build up the community organization which the Christians there still lacked. Titus was to stay on the island of Crete until Artemas or Tychicus came to relieve him (3:12). Then he was to come quickly to Nicopolis (in Epirus), where Paul was spending the winter (3:12).

In his letter to Titus, the Apostle designated the two tasks which his deputy was to perform on the island: to organize the life of the church, and to combat false teachers. Paul may have written this letter at the same time as his First Epistle to Timothy (c. 65 AD); it was probably delivered by Zenas and Apollos (3:13).

Paul had probably only worked for a short time with Titus in Crete, preaching the gospel and establishing Christian communities. In any case, he himself had only laid the foundations for these communities, and on his departure from the island he left Titus behind to complete the work of building them up (1:5). Especially important in this respect was the appointment of supervisors, presbyters, in each community—a task Paul expressly delegated to Titus. Paul demanded that certain qualities, which he carefully enumerated (1:6–9), be apparent in men chosen for this position. They must be true believers, morally mature, and well disciplined, men obedient to God and ready to serve their brethren in love (1 : 6–9). Paul also gave Titus clear instructions about how Christians from within the various classes and conditions should lead their lives.

The Apostle's authority was there to support the words of Titus, who was perhaps still only a young man. He gave him directions concerning the older men (2:2) and the older women (2:3). He tells the duties of the young women (2:4–5) and of the young men (2:6). He points out to him the important task of the slaves in the Christian community (2:9f.). He describes briefly the right attitude of Christians to the pagan authorities (3:1), and indicates how they should behave in their pagan and often downright repulsive environment (3:2). On two occasions he emphasizes the importance of the Christian way of life as an example to the Jews and pagans outside their community. The young women are to lead an exemplary life, so that "the word of God may not be discredited" (2:5), and the slaves are to serve obediently and faithfully "so that in everything they may adorn the doctrine of God our Saviour" (2:10).

We notice again and again in St. Paul's letters that the proclamation of our salvation is linked indissolubly with moral exhortation—we find this, too, in the Epistle to Titus. In 2:1–10 he has listed the duties of each particular class, and he later points to their source of strength for the Christian life. The demands made on them are related to the salvation they have received. For the grace of God, which became man in Jesus Christ, has bestowed salvation on them through faith and baptism (2:11). This grace of God draws Christians to make a profound break with all godlessness and evil desires, and to practice a true Christian life towards God, their neighbor, and themselves (2:12). The foundation stone of such a life is hope in "the appearing of the glory of our great God and Saviour

Jesus Christ," hope in the second coming of the risen Lord (2:13). Surrendering himself to death on the cross, Jesus Christ ransomed Christians from their servitude to sin and death. He purified them and made of them a chosen, holy race; as he did to God's people of the old covenant, he purified, chose, and sanctified them as his people of the new covenant, who, "zealous for good deeds" (2:14), must now lead a truly Christian life.

Having concluded the requirements for the right ordering of life (3:2), the Apostle again points out that the basis of a morally good life is the salvation we have received. The Christians of Crete can all the more readily and willingly show patient forgiveness and self-sacrificing love towards their pagan fellow citizens when they think of the change that took place in their own lives only a short time ago with their conversion to Christianity. At one time, they were no better than those pagan men, but now in baptism, "by the washing of regeneration and renewal in the Holy Spirit, which he has poured out upon them richly through Jesus Christ our Saviour," they have received salvation. That was made possible by God's great deed, which dawned in the birth of Jesus Christ and his death on the cross (3:4-6). Made holy in this way through baptism and the Holy Spirit, Christians are already heirs to the eternal life they hope for (3:7). In these words taken, we can suppose, from an early Christian baptismal hymn, the work of the Trinity is portrayed: God's work of grace in Christian man. In the exclusion of all human praise and merit, God's act of pure graciousness stands out in strong relief (3:5-7). Because they have received this saving gift, Christians have a duty to be active in good works. In the midst of a pagan world they must "apply themselves to good deeds." So, on both occasions, the Apostle's moral exhortation to the Christians of the young communities is intimately bound up with his declaration of the salvation they have received.

The second duty Titus has to perform in the churches of Crete is to oppose false teachers. There are already a lot of these men present in the communities, but we are not told whether they are infiltrators from outside, or whether, as is more probable, they have risen from within the community (1:10). They are portrayed as disobedient, unruly people (1:10) who oppose the Apostle, his teachings, and directives. They are empty talkers, for what they proclaim is baseless (1:10); they are deceivers, for their teaching claims a higher knowledge (1:16) and a strict, ascetic view of life (1:10, 14). The "circumcision party," the Judaeo-Christians, are especially ardent champions of this false doctrine. They do not restrict their activity to individual Christians, but confuse whole families (1:11) and so constitute a menace to the churches (1:11). A distinctive light is thrown on their ethical conduct by the fact that they spread their false teachings out of a base desire for profit (1:11). They turn their preaching into a business enterprise.

The teachings they spread are not clearly and plainly described here. They look like the false doctrines we meet with in the First and Second Epistles to Timothy. They are concerned with Jewish myths (1:14), with speculations about genealogies (3:9), with commands of men, especially with regulations about food and purification (1:14; 3:9), the absurdity of which the Apostle reveals in plain and forthright language (1:15). They boast of a higher knowledge of God (1:16), but their unchristian life strongly contradicts this. From the various statements in the letter to Titus, then, the basic ideas of the false teaching appear to be on the one hand the claim to a higher knowledge of God, and on the other hand the demand for a strict, ascetic attitude to life. We have here very probably something similar to what we find in the first and second letters to Timothy, a form of early Judaeo-gnostic doctrinal error of the sort that also confronts us in the letter to the Colossians (Col. 2:16–18).

Titus must fight the danger threatening the faith of the Cretan churches with the greatest determination. He must silence the false teachers (1:11) and prevent the propagation of their teaching especially in the public assemblies. He must take vigorous steps against them, for the danger to the Christian communities is all the greater in that the subversive activity of the false teachers is facilitated by the moral weakness of the Cretan people (1:12). Cretans were known to be untruthful, coarse, and lazy and the Apostle frankly confirms their reputation (1:13). For this reason it is essential that his deputy intervene strongly (3:8). Titus must not engage in any theological discussions or controversies about the false teaching; he must simply reject and shun it, for it is useless and pernicious (3:9). Paul also gives his deputy quite definite directives for the treatment of false teachers: if he has warned a man once or twice and not been heeded, he must break off relations with him and avoid further contact (3:10). For it is not up to Titus to pass judgment on such a man; the false teacher's own conscience is his judge (3:11).

In all these tasks Titus must prove himself by his exemplary Christian life and proclamation of the gospel message. The life of the community will flourish all the more if the pastor's life is a shining and untarnished model for it, and his preaching ardent and forceful. So his example must light the way in every good deed (2:7). He must only preach what is according to "sound doctrine," the doctrine of the gospel, the pure and unadulterated truth of revelation (2:1). He is to speak, admonish, and reprove "with all authority," without fear or hesitation (2 : 15). He is to bear insistent witness to the saving acts of God (3 : 8). In preaching, he is to be a model and example; in teaching, he is to show himself incorruptible and dignified, sound and unassailable in his words (2 : 7f.). If Titus does his duty in this way, his opponents in the Christian community, and even more so those outside it, will be disconcerted, not being able to find anything bad to say of him (2 : 8). Indeed, the Apostle himself places his whole authority behind Titus, and requires of the Christians that they do not disregard or despise his deputy (2 : 15). Even though Titus learns through this very letter that he is soon to be relieved from his round of duties by Artemas or Tychicus (3 : 12), he must, as the "true child" of the Apostle, continue until that time comes to perform those same duties which Paul has characterized at the beginning of his letter as the proper tasks of the apostolate: to preserve and propagate the Christian faith by establishing order in the life of the Church, and by combatting the false teachers (1 : 1).

OUTLINE

The Opening of the Letter (1 : 1–4)

OPENING ADDRESS (1 : 1–4)

I. The writer (1 : 1a)

II. The Apostle's duties (1 : 1b–3)

III. The addressees (1 : 4a)

IV. Greeting (1 : 4b)

The Body of the Letter (1 : 5—3 : 11)

TITUS'S DUTIES IN CRETE (1 : 5–16)

  I. The appointment of presbyters and their distinctive qualities (1 : 5–9)

    1. The appointment of presbyters (1 : 5)

    2. The qualities necessary in a presbyter (1 : 6–9)

  II. The campaign against the false teachers (1 : 10–16)

    1. Description of the false teachers (1 : 10–11)

    2. Errors and vices of the Cretans (1 : 12–13)

    3. Characteristics of the false teaching (1 : 14–16)

THE CHRISTIAN LIFE (2 : 1—3 : 11)

  I. Duties of the various classes (2 : 1–10)

    1. Preaching sound doctrine (2 : 1)

    2. Duties of the older men and older women (2 : 2–3)

    3. Duties of the young women and young men (2 : 4–6)

    4. Titus's own example (2 : 7–8)

    5. Duties of the slaves (2 : 9–10)

THE OPENING OF THE LETTER
(1:1-4)

OPENING ADDRESS (1:1–4)

The Writer (1:1a)

¹ªPaul, a servant of God and an apostle of Jesus Christ . . .

In contrast to the two other pastoral epistles, the First and
Second Epistles to Timothy, the opening address of the Epistle
to Titus is longer and more solemn; indeed there are certain
similarities with the Epistle to the Romans. As in that letter,
the simple form of greeting common in antiquity is extended by
important additions in which the tasks of an apostle of Jesus
Christ are briefly expounded (1:1b), and reference is made to
hope in eternal life as the cornerstone of the apostolate (1:2–3).
Paul's letter is addressed to one of his most faithful disciples
and co-workers, and yet he speaks of himself as being God's
"servant," his "slave," and lays stress on his dignity as an
apostle. This is because it is not a private letter to Titus that we
have here, but an official document. It is, to be sure, addressed
formally to Titus, but it is intended for all the Christians of
Crete, and most probably for public reading at their eucharistic
assemblies. It is necessary that the authority of the Apostle and
of his deputy Titus be strongly emphasized if they are to achieve
an intensive build-up of communities on the island and a decisive
rejection of the false teachers. Paul is *God's servant;* he belongs
to him entirely; he must surrender his whole life to him, and
all his work. Conversely, this description means that like the
leaders of the Israelites, like Abraham, Moses, David, Isaiah,

3

he has been singled out for a special service, a special mission.

In relation to Christ he is an *apostle,* Christ's envoy endowed with full powers to proclaim the message of his word. So this saying of Jesus is true of Paul: "As the Father has sent me, even so I send you" (Jn. 20:21). Behind Titus stands the whole authority of the Apostle to the Gentiles; behind Paul stands Christ himself and God. From God and Christ something is to be imparted to the community. So it is that the Christians of Crete are called upon in receiving the letter to receive the word of God and of his fully authorized ambassador.

The Apostle's Duties (1:1b–3)

1b. *. . . to further the faith of God's elect and their knowledge of the truth which accords with godliness . . .*

Paul has a twofold mission as apostle. First of all, he has to keep and preserve "God's elect" in the Christian faith. God has singled out the Christians from the rest of mankind and by his grace called them to believe. As he is to state later on, danger is now threatening from the ranks of the false teachers. So already at the beginning of his letter he points out one of its important aims: to *confirm and strengthen* the Christians in their faith against all the false teachings which are being propagated on the island. For Paul realizes that, as the Lord's apostle, he is responsible for the continued preservation of the Christian faith in the communities.

Paul's second mission as apostle is concerned with spreading the *knowledge of the truth which accords with godliness.* "Godliness" means here, as it does in the First Epistle to Timothy, the faith of the church as opposed to the doctrines of the false teachers (1 Tim. 6:3; cf. 3:6). Paul, then, is appointed to proclaim and promulgate true knowledge of the Christian faith. If men are to come to true belief, God's call is necessary, but necessary, too, is the Apostle's preaching of the truth that is revealed. Through this preaching Paul will lead men to realize and see for themselves the saving truth of Christianity. To the Apostle this is a compelling duty, which makes him cry out: " Woe to me if I do not preach the gospel!" (1 Cor. 9:16).

[2]. . . *in hope of eternal life which God, who never lies, promised ages ago* . . .

In both these tasks—seeing that the communities receive the faith and keep it, as well as his apostolic work of spreading Christian truth—Paul falls back on the *hope of eternal life.* That is the firm basis of his life and work; that is the good news he proclaims to all Christians (cf. 2 Tim. 1:1), so that their life, too, may rest on this unshakable foundation.

But is it possible for life to be founded on such a hope? Is this " hope of eternal life " not a human chimera and hallucination? The Apostle answers: *God himself* stands as assurance of this eternal life and of this hope. He who can neither lie nor deceive, he who has shown himself right through the saving history of the old covenant to be the true and faithful God, has " ages ago," in times long past, promised eternal life when he laid down the decree of our redemption. From paradise and throughout the course of salvation history a whole chain of prophetic promises has pointed to the goal of the old covenant, to Christ. He brings eternal life; he is eternal life.

[3a]. . . *and at the proper time manifested in his word through the preaching* . . .

At the proper time, then, the time set in his decree (1 Tim. 2:6), God has unveiled the mystery. Through Jesus Christ he has revealed his word, the word which contains and guarantees the promise of eternal life (cf. 2 Tim. 1:9f.). At this moment in time God's silence is broken through Jesus Christ, the Word made man, and the saving gift of eternal life is made known to all mankind.

³ᵇ. . . *with which I have been entrusted by command of God our Saviour;. . .*

Paul was chosen out and destined by God's grace to preach this good news when he was called to be the Apostle of the Gentiles (1 Tim. 1:11). This, then, is the sublime task, the high responsibility of his apostolate: to make known to all men God's promise of eternal life revealed and made available in Jesus Christ: to those who believe, that they may stand firm in their faith and form their lives by it; to those who do not believe, that they may come to faith. His hearers, for their part, must open their hearts to his preaching so that God's word may bear fruit, the word of his plan, in which he shows himself to be the *Saviour and Redeemer* of mankind.

The Addressees (1:4a)

⁴ᵃ. . . *To Titus, my true child in a common faith :* . . .

Only now, after he has dealt with the tasks of his apostolate and its raison d'être, does he name the letter's recipient, Titus, for whom he shows the same love he has for Timothy, calling him

" my true child in a common faith " (cf. 1 Tim. 1:2). It was
Paul who had led him to the faith, won him for Christianity;
so he can justifiably call him his " child," and refer to their
relationship as that of father to son. He is his *true child* in that
he nourishes the same way of thinking as his spiritual father to
whom he is bound in love and loyalty. The same bond of
Christian faith unites them both. Can the Apostle say anything
more for Titus than he does in calling him his " true child "?
All Christians should be bound together in true brotherhood
through the faith they share, just as Paul and Titus were.

Greeting (1:4b)

[4b]. . . *Grace and peace from God the Father and Christ Jesus
our Saviour.*

Instead of the usual Greek greeting (" joy ") or the Jewish one
(" peace "), the Apostle wishes the recipient of his letter " grace
and peace." He raises the customary common greeting of the
day to a Christian plane, desiring what is for the Christian the
most important thing: *grace,* God's inexhaustible good favor,
and *peace,* the healing given by a loving father. These saving
gifts have their source in God alone and in Jesus Christ, who
stands with him as Son and risen Lord. This greeting is no
empty wish, but an effective bestowal on Titus of the whole
fullness of God's favor and of his salvation. God stands as
assurance of this as our loving " Father," and Jesus Christ as
" our Saviour."

THE BODY OF THE LETTER
(1:5—3:11)

TITUS'S DUTIES IN CRETE (1:5–16)

In many of Paul's letters we can distinguish two parts: the Apostle first of all recalls and manifests God's saving work, and then he draws out the consequences for the Christian life. In contrast to this, the letter to Titus, like the two other pastoral epistles, exhibits a looser sort of division. Here the author has two main concerns: on the one hand, the ordering of church life in the Cretan communities; on the other, the struggle against false teachers. The instructions Paul gives his fellow worker, who is now his deputy on the island, are arranged only in a loose order. Titus is to complete the work begun by the Apostle in building up the Christian communities, and above all he is to appoint supervisors in the individual churches (1:5–9). He also gives him detailed directives about church order and about the Christian life (2:1—3:7). And, beyond all this, Paul wants to encourage Titus by his letter to be firm and decisive in his campaign against the false teachers in the communities (1:10–16; 3:8–11). In this confrontation, Titus's position is that of deputy to the Apostle who is the overall leader of all the churches, a position Paul strengthens and underpins with all the power of his word as an apostle. So it is that in the first part of his letter he is concerned to show the tasks Titus must perform in Crete: he must appoint supervisors in each community, men from whom special qualities are demanded (1:5–9); and then he must do battle with the false teachers, the devotees of Jewish myths and human precepts (1:10–16).

The Appointment of Presbyters
and Their Distinctive Qualities (1:5–9)

The Appointment of Presbyters (1:5)

⁵*This is why I left you in Crete, that you might amend what was defective, and appoint elders in every town as I directed you, . . .*

After he had been set free from his first Roman captivity, Paul could only have worked for a short time along with Titus in Crete (*c.* 63/64 AD). We have no further information about this activity of the Apostle. The island was at that time well populated, and the faith had found a foothold in many towns. Paul had, of course, only been able to lay the foundations for the churches. We know nothing of the extent to which the gospel had been introduced into the island before this missionary journey of his. Nor do we know why Paul left the island so soon, before the formation of the individual communities had been fully achieved. On his departure, he left Titus behind with exceptionally far-reaching authority. He was to complete the work which remained of building up the individual groups, bring order into the relationships within them, and so " amend what is defective " there.

The Apostle had enjoined another particularly responsible task on Titus when he left. He must *appoint presbyters,* supervisors for the community, in every town where one had been established. The communities are not themselves to nominate these men from their own ranks: the task of doing so is laid on Titus. This is a well-founded precaution, considering how young the churches on the island are. We see again and again in Paul's letters how extensively the Apostle calls upon his fellow workers, entrusting them with difficult and highly responsible commissions. So here, too, he has full confidence that Titus, his " true child in a common faith," will bring this difficult business to a satisfactory conclusion.

The Qualities Necessary in a Presbyter (1:6 9)

Definite principles must be observed in the choice of presbyters. The Apostle may merely be repeating here in writing what he had outlined verbally to his deputy before his departure. As in 1 Timothy 3:2–7, he lists the qualities demanded of one who is to bear this office. We must realize that conditions on Crete, where the churches were still very young, were somewhat different from those in Ephesus, where the faith had been accepted some time ago. The Apostle, being a wise and experienced pastor, takes into consideration the actual stage reached by the communities from whose ranks the presbyters are to be chosen. Nevertheless, the list of required qualities accords verbally in part with that in 1 Timothy 3:2–7. Though the formulation is different in the letter to Titus, the sense is the same.

6a. . . if any man is blameless, the husband of one wife, . . .

In his choice of supervisors for the churches, Titus must take two primary factors into account. In the first place, the man chosen must be of blameless repute. There must be no stain on the character of one who is to be worthy and deserving of the church's trust. Verse 7 expresses negatively, and verse 8 positively, all that is involved in such a life. When the supervisor of the community is required to be " the husband of one wife," this would seem to mean not that his married life should be free of even the slightest stigma, but that he is no longer allowed to contract a second marriage after his wife's death. The Apostle expressly allows Christians in general to enter a second marriage, but he lays this high demand on the leader of the community— a demand which is, as it were, a first step towards the ideal of celibacy enjoined as obligatory on her ministers by the church of later ages.

[6b]. . . *and his children are believers and not open to the charge of being profligate or insubordinate.*

The second important factor is a man's *exemplary family life.* In these early days, the church's ministers were married men; celibacy, the obligation not to marry, was not introduced until later. In the young churches of Crete, it could easily happen that only the parents would be converted to the faith, their children remaining unbelievers. That is why the Apostle demands of the " elders " that their children, too, be Christians. But that is not enough. The children must not bring their father into ill repute by disorderly and undisciplined conduct or disobedience, which would make his ministry impossible. The father, then, in his family and household, is to be a model for the Christian church. For the minister must be able to show in his small family circle that he is a sound master of his own household who can bring up his children to be honorable, obedient, and self-controlled. How could a man who fails to lead his own family well be entrusted with the greater family of the local church and all its needs?

⁷For a bishop, as God's steward, must be blameless; he must not be arrogant or quick-tempered or a drunkard or violent or greedy for gain, . . .

It is noticeable that the Apostle goes on to call "bishop" (*episkopos*) the same official who has up to this point been called a "presbyter." This shows that the designation of the grades of hierarchy had not yet been firmly fixed. Both terms (" presbyter " and " bishop ") were used alongside each other with exactly the same meaning; both referred to the minister, the supervisor of the community.

We go on to hear about what is incompatible with the blameless life of a minister. He, the " bishop," is " God's steward " (cf. 1 Cor. 4:1), for he must see to the ordering of the church which is " the household of God " (1 Tim. 3:15), just as the householder and the steward do in an ordinary house (cf. Lk. 12:42f.). It is very clear from the picture painted that the office of supervisor in the church is no lordship over men but a *true serving* before God. So only he has a place at the head of the community who is a faithful and reliable instrument in God's service. Therefore all self-seeking, rebelliousness, greed for profit, and arrogance, must be entirely absent from the personal conduct of one who bears this office. Unchristian dispositions such as these would defile the ministry the presbyter must perform.

⁸. . . but hospitable, a lover of goodness, master of himself, upright, holy, and self-controlled; . . .

Now, in contrast, a positive picture is given of the genuine Christian attitude a minister must show. Time after time in the writings of the New Testament, Christians are called upon to exercise hospitality to their children who are traveling through from different parts. So it stands to reason that the presbyter's house should have an ever-open door for Christians who are on a journey or are suffering and in need of help: the keynote must be *loving service*. The presbyter must be a man of wisdom, upright and godly, self-controlled and mature, who stands firm in the ways of goodness.

⁹. . . *he must hold firm to the sure word as taught, so that he may be able to give instruction in sound doctrine and also to confute those who contradict it.*

The Apostle leaves the most important requirement to the end of his list: the supervisor in the community must *hold firm to the sure word as taught,* the traditional faith of the church. As the apostolic age draws to a close and the generation of eye-witnesses and hearers of Jesus' words and deeds dies out, the work of handing down the Lord's untarnished words and teaching becomes all the more important. It is the handing on of the apostolic tradition which lives on in the church, and which in the other two pastoral epistles the Apostle calls " the truth that has been entrusted to you " (2 Tim. 1:14; cf. 1 Tim. 6:20; 2 Tim. 1: 12). Preaching this " sure word " is a central part of the presbyter's ministry. This apostolic tradition alone is the " sound doctrine " (1 Tim. 1:10). It is the touchstone, the norm by which all preaching in the church must be judged. Only when the leader of the community takes his stand on this firm ground, only when he proclaims this revelation of God, is he in a position to instruct and admonish the Christians; only then has he the ability to rebuke " those who contradict it," the false teachers who are confusing the community.

When one considers the particular demands the Apostle makes on the leaders of the churches in their ministry, one realizes that he has in mind men of high moral standing, disciplined men who are firm in their faith and prepared in all things to serve God in obedient love. It is noticeable here that Paul does not mention as his conditions the sort of qualities we so readily demand: outstanding gifts, brilliant powers of oratory, sophistication, organizing ability, good relationships with men of influence. To him the important thing is that a man be prepared to obey God and serve him and the brethren in love—and this readiness is the fruit of a strong, untarnished *faith*.

The Apostle's allusion to " those who contradict " gives us the keynote for what follows.

The Campaign Against the False Teachers (1:10–16)

In the preceding paragraph, Paul referred to the duty of the minister in the community to take his stand on the firm ground of traditional faith, and to correct the false teachers who oppose him. Now he goes on to describe these false teachers.

Description of the False Teachers (1:10–11)

[10]*For there are many insubordinate men, empty talkers and deceivers, especially the circumcision party; [11]they must be silenced, since they are upsetting whole families by teaching for base gain what they have no right to teach.*

There is already a large number of false teachers in the churches of Crete, which are still not very firm in their faith. Perhaps they

came across from Asia Minor and, following in the footsteps of
the Apostle as he preached the gospel, gained entry into the
infant churches. Or maybe they arose from within these churches
themselves, weak as they still were in their faith. They are portrayed as *insubordinate men*. They do indeed belong to the
church but oppose its teaching and organization, and refuse to
submit to it.

The Apostle scornfully calls them *empty talkers,* for all their
teaching contains is hollow rumor. But they are dangerous men
too, *deceivers* whose teaching, to judge by its effects, is a bewil-
dering, seductive delusion. For it lays claim to a higher form of
knowledge and a strict, ascetic outlook on life. The " circumcision party," the Judaeo-Christians, are in the forefront of this
movement. These men represent a real danger to the church, so
a firm and energetic stand is called for. Titus must " silence "
them. He must prevent them from coming forward to teach,
especially in church assemblies. For there is great danger that by
their false teaching they may bring about the downfall not only
of individual Christians but also of whole families, and thereby
cause untold damage in the community.

Clear light is shed on their morals by the Apostle's statement
that it is out of desire for *base gain* that they teach the doctrines
" they have no right to teach." They know how to exploit their
followers, and their preaching is for them at the same time a
lucrative *business* (cf. 1 Tim. 6:6–8). It was the general custom
at that time to provide the church's ministers with their live-
lihood through voluntary gifts and contributions. This gave to an
unscrupulous and avaricious preacher in the community many an
opportunity for self-enrichment. That is why Paul demands so
forcibly that a minister be selfless, and why he inveighs so
strongly against the greed of the false teachers.

Here too, in the Christian communities of Crete, the weeds have appeared which the enemy has sown among the wheat. Here the Lord's parable has come true (Mt. 13:24–30). In whatever field the good seed is sown, the enemy will come and sow weeds along with it. And when the seed grows and bears fruit, the weeds too will appear.

Errors and Vices of the Cretans (1:12–13)

¹²*One of themselves, a prophet of their own, said, " Cretans are always liars, evil beasts, lazy gluttons." ¹³This testimony is true. Therefore rebuke them sharply, that they may be sound in the faith, . . .*

The false teachers have their work of subversion made all the easier by the *moral weakness* of the Cretan people. In evidence of this, the Apostle cites a verse from the poem *On the Sayings of the Oracle* by their famous countryman Epimenides. This work of the sixth century BC is known only in fragments, but the words he quotes had already become a well-known saying. He refers to the way the Cretans themelves looked on this poet as a " prophet," such was his fame in antiquity. The verse in question names three vices of theirs: untruthfulness, which was legendary in those days, brutishness, and idleness. Paul is not content merely to cite the blunt words of the poet, but states plainly and frankly that he finds this rather unattractive portrayal of the Cretan character confirmed by what he has experienced of the Christian communities there.

The Apostle is of the opinion that only sharp, unyielding reproof will serve any purpose here. Titus must intervene without hesitation wherever Christians are showing signs of giving way to the false teaching. Only if he does so will they become *sound in the faith,* preserving the true and incorrupt belief of the gospel; for only this traditional teaching is the " sound doctrine " (1 Tim. 1 : 10) as opposed to the false; only this exhibits the spiritual and moral health which leads to a virtuous life. The Apostle describes unsparingly the great danger which threatens the Christian churches on the island. He loves his Christian children like a mother (cf. Gal. 5 : 19), but when he sees their faith in jeopardy he is capable of being hard and stern in his demands.

Characteristics of the False Teaching (1:14–16)

14. . . . .*instead of giving heed to Jewish myths or to commands of men who reject the truth.*

Two aspects of the false teaching are now briefly described. Paul's statement that one of its concerns is Jewish myths leaves us wondering what sort of myths he means. We can be sure anyway that they are rabbinic fables of some kind, with no foundation in truth. As in the First Epistle to Timothy, it is most probably a question of fantastic stories and speculations about Old Testament texts and genealogies, all said to possess some deep, hidden sense. The Jewish origin of these ideas is clear (1 : 10; 3 : 9), but they show traces of the later, very pernicious error of gnosticism (1 : 16). A second characteristic of the false teaching is that its followers pay heed to " commands of men who reject the truth." The next verse shows clearly that this refers to the observance of Jewish regulations about food and purification.

¹⁵*To the pure all things are pure, but to the corrupt and un-
believing nothing is pure; their very minds and consciences are
corrupt.*

The Apostle now goes into the question of these " commands of
men who reject the truth," the question of the rules about food
and purification. He confronts them tersely with words whose
power lies in their crystal clarity : *to the pure all things are pure.*
These words echo the saying of Jesus : " Hear me, all of you,
and understand : there is nothing outside a man which by
going into him can defile him; but the things which come out of
a man are what defile him " (Mk. 7 : 14f.). This was a firm conviction among the Christian churches (cf. Rom. 14 : 14–20) : that
no creature is evil to him who has been washed clean by God in
baptism (cf. 3 : 5–7) and is pure in heart and mind. Everything
we come across in the course of our activity, our employment or
our recreation, is pure for us if we are pure in our inmost being
and deepest sentiments. The Christian of whom this is true may
use God's gifts with the freedom he has as God's child. " For
everything created by God is good " (1 Tim. 4 : 4), and, as he
himself made plain to Peter in a vision (cf. Acts 10 : 1–16), his
creation, redeemed by Jesus Christ, is not unclean. The Christian
who is aware of this should be joyful in his use of all creation's
gifts.

So the false teachings, the " commands of men," offend
against the order of God's creative and redemptive work : they
reject the truth. If, on the other hand, a man's attitude, his
conscience, is " corrupted," everything is unclean for him. He
can misuse and desecrate what is noblest and most beautiful :
his bad conscience and perverted way of thinking will lead him
to turn it to the sinful satisfaction of his greed. Purity is a ques-

tion of one's attitude of heart; it does not lie within Nature itself. This inner disposition is the decisive factor, the living center of one's moral life. So the strict, ascetic views of the false teachers contradict the good news of the true gospel: they " reject the truth."

[16]*They profess to know God, but they deny him by their deeds; they are detestable, disobedient, unfit for any good deed.*

A further characteristic of the false teaching is its claim to a *higher knowledge of God.* This clearly indicates its affinity with the later, very dangerous error of gnosticism. The Apostle refutes the claim briefly and concisely. The proof of one's knowledge of God is, he says, one's practical Christian life, and this holds for the false teachers too. If you say that you know God, but disown him in your daily life and action, you are an abomination to him: " He who says ' I know him ' but disobeys his commandments is a liar, and the truth is not in him " (1 Jn. 2:4).

Two assertions appear, then, as central to the false teaching: its claim to a higher knowledge of God, and its strict, ascetic outlook on life. Paul rejects both assertions brusquely. The false teachers are in his eyes " detestable " and " disobedient " because of their rebellious, insubordinate attitude to God and to the true message of his good news. For that reason, too, they are " unfit for any good deed."

THE CHRISTIAN LIFE (2:1—3:11)

Besides completing the formation of the Christian communities on the island of Crete, and appointing presbyters with the necessary qualities in the individual churches (1:5-9), Titus has the further task of seeing that his people live an orderly Christian life. So he is to preach what is in accordance with the "sound," healthy doctrine of the Christian message, and show the various classes and conditions among the Christians what their duties are. He is himself to lead the way for them as a shining example of all that is good. The source of strength for this Christian life is God's grace, made manifest in Jesus Christ (2:11-15). The Apostle outlines the duties of a Christian towards the authorities and towards his fellow men (3:1-2). Then he speaks again of God's mercy, which has been revealed in our redemption through Jesus Christ and made open to us in the washing of regeneration and renewal in the Holy Spirit. And he points thereby to the possibility of Christians excelling in good works, for they are heirs to eternal life (3:3-8). He concludes the letter proper with another warning against the false teaching and a directive about the treatment of those who are promoting it (3:9-11).

Duties of the Various Classes (2:1-10)

Preaching Sound Doctrine (2:1)

¹*But as for you, teach what befits sound doctrine.*

Paul has given a sharp warning against the false teachers in Crete (1 : 10–16). They preach " Jewish myths " and " commands of men "; Titus, on the contrary, must preach " what befits sound doctrine." The Apostle calls the gospel teaching the *sound doctrine*: it is the pure and undistorted word of revelation, the perfect expression of spiritual and moral health, producing in its turn a pure and healthy life. Whatever, then, contradicts this teaching is unhealthy; it contains the germs of sickness and leads to an immoral life. That is why Titus must preach only what accords with the good news of Jesus Christ. He must draw his words only from the pure well-spring of God's revelation (cf. 1 Tim. 6:20; 2 Tim. 1:14). In like manner, every Christian preacher is bound in his preaching to the " sound doctrine," the revealed word of Jesus Christ. His duty is to preserve it carefully and hand it down without adding to it or suppressing any part of it. Jesus bequeathed the Holy Spirit to his church as the pledge of his truth, and it is the Holy Spirit who guarantees that the word of revelation remains pure and uncontaminated in the church (cf. Jn. 16:13).

Now the Apostle lays down in detail how the " sound doctrine " should form the Christian life of the various classes.

Duties of the Older Men and Older Women (2 :2–3)

²*Bid the older men be temperate, serious, sensible, sound in faith, in love, and in steadfastness.* ³*Bid the older women likewise to be reverent in behavior, not to be slanderers or slaves to drink; they are to teach what is good, . . .*

The Apostle begins with the older men. Mellow and mature in character, they should show their mastery of all life's difficulties, and prove themselves by their sobriety, their reserved and temperate indulgence in wine, their respectability, their dignified, manly appearance, their level-headedness, and their self-control. The basic Christian attitudes of *faith, love,* and *steadfastness* should be especially evident in their lives.

The older women must, in their inner attitude and outer behavior, show all the dignity of mature Christians. They must respect their fellow men by controlling their tongue and avoiding all slanderous talk. It is noticeable how Paul warns them seriously to be moderate in their drinking habits. Perhaps he had had some unpleasant experience in this respect, or had some particular event in mind, especially as Crete was a famous country for wine. Through their experience of life and through their Christ-like example they are to *teach what is good* to the younger women; that is, after all, the proper task of the mature. The Apostle's instructions are no more than a repetition of the demands Jesus made in his Sermon on the Mount: " Let your light so shine before men, that they may see your good works and give glory to your Father who is in heaven " (Mt. 5:16).

Duties of the Young Women and Young Men (2:4-6)

. . . and so train the young women to love their husbands and children, ⁵to be sensible, chaste, domestic, kind, and submissive to their husbands, that the word of God may not be discredited. ⁶Likewise urge the younger men to control themselves.

Paul requires the young women to be good wives and mothers. He draws an inspiring portrait of the Christian woman who is entirely devoted to her vocation as wife and mother in her household. She is sensible, honorable and kind-hearted. Her life is founded on love for her husband and her children, and she performs all her duties in reverent submission to her husband. These qualities are, of course, not exclusively Christian virtues; the Apostle is concerned to show concretely how Christian faith must be effective in a woman's daily life. We must realize too that Paul takes as his starting point the social position of women at that time, and that position cannot be compared with the present-day one.

If a woman leads her life in this way, giving a public example to the pagans around her of what a really Christian life involves, she will never give the enemies of Christianity among them an opportunity to scorn the faith. Nor, in a mixed marriage, will her daily life ever give rise to disparaging judgments about Christianity by her pagan husband. Indeed, she may bring it about that " some, though they do not obey the word, may be won without a word by the behavior of their wives " (1 Pet. 3:1).

The young men are admonished very briefly to *control themselves* and be prudent in all things. The ideal of Christian youth is contrasted with the tendency they may have to rush impetuously and passionately into life and into frivolous company. So it is that each member of the church has the duty, a holy duty, of setting an example to the community by his Christian life, and of bringing honor to the faith from the Jews and pagans beyond its bounds.

Titus's Own Example (2:7–8)

⁷Show yourself in all respects a model of good deeds, and in your teaching show integrity, gravity, ⁸and sound speech that

cannot be censured, so that an opponent may be put to shame,
having nothing evil to say of us.

Paul interrupts his instructions for the various classes of
Christians, and now turns to Titus himself. His *own example*
is more important than all his preaching and exhortation. So he
must lead the way as the model of all good deeds. His preaching
must be of the pure gospel message, spoken with sentiments
which are noble and clear for everyone to see. And he must
show due gravity, preaching only with " sound speech that cannot be censured." Again the author uses the word " sound " to
describe the pure, untainted gospel teaching (cf. 2:1), which
" cannot be censured " because it is wholly based on what has
been revealed. Titus must be so exemplary in his life and in his
preaching that all his adversaries within the church, like the
false teachers for instance, and even more so all those outside it,
will be forced into embarrassed silence, not being able to find
the fuel they are always looking for in Christianity for their
campaigns. Again Paul makes reference to the good example
Titus must give not only in the church but also to those outside
it (cf. 2:5). He must shine as a light before men, and always
take care to give scandal to no one (cf. Mt. 5:16; 18:7).

Duties of the Slaves (2:9–10)

[9]*Bid slaves to be submissive to their masters and to give satisfac-*
tion in every respect; they are not to be refractory, [10]*not to pilfer,*
but to show entire and true fidelity, so that in everything they
may adorn the doctrine of God our Saviour.

Paul now turns his attention to a final group in the church, that of the Christian slaves, who often have to live and work in pagan households in the midst of the pagan world. They too have an important task to perform, although their position is much despised. It is significant that the Apostle (as he does in 1 Tim. 6: 1–2) gives his deputy precise directives about this group. Their Christian life, their obedience and good-heartedness, their loyalty, reliability, and absolute honesty towards their master, even if he be a pagan, must make them truly *adorn the Christian faith*. In this way they prove themselves the redeemed of God, who is himself our Saviour, in that he is the final reason for the redemption of mankind. " It pleased God through the folly of what we preach to save those who believe " (1 Cor. 1 : 21). Paul does not for the time being want to revoke the legal relationship of slave to master which was in force at that time; he has no program for re-structuring society. But he does point out to the slaves that they have a great and important work to do in the church. Despite their lowly position, they are to be a jewel in the garment of the Christian faith.

We must be struck by the fact that in this section of his letter (2: 1–10), the Apostle speaks three times about good example (2:5, 8, 10). It is always the case that the best defense of the Christian faith is a genuinely *Christian life*; one which grows out of true, sincerely held belief, and is ready to serve in devotion to duty and self-sacrificing love.

God's Grace as Fount of Strength (2:11–15)

Where, then, are these various classes of people in the Cretan church going to find the strength they need for the Christian

life, whose demands the Apostle has just laid down for them
(2:1-10)? Paul replies: In the grace of God which has appeared
in Jesus Christ (2:11), and which even here on earth raises up
the Christian to a life of holiness (2:12). The cornerstone of such
a life is hope in the second coming of Jesus Christ (2:13). The
twofold work of God's grace is portrayed as the fulfillment of the
Old Testament promise (2:14). Titus must proclaim this message
that our strength is in God's grace (2:15).

God's Grace Revealed in Jesus Christ (2:11–14)

¹¹*For the grace of God has appeared for the salvation of all
men,* . . .

Paul bursts out now into a great song in praise of God's loving
kindness and his grace. At the time appointed in God's saving
plan, his unfathomable *graciousness and love* appeared in Jesus
Christ; they became man in his only-begotten Son. He who is
both God and man is God's gracious love in person. In him God
offers salvation to all men without exception. For he " so loved
the world that he gave his only Son, that whoever believes in
him should not perish but have eternal life " (Jn. 3:16). That is
the goal all men have to reach: salvation from eternal death, the
enjoyment of eternal life. God's good favor knows no bounds.
In Jesus Christ he offers salvation to all men, irrespective of person, social class, or race. We cannot grasp this love of his, this
love which has taken its decisive stand in time and in eternity.
But we do know that it compels us to make our own clear-cut
decision: to open ourselves to the call of his love, or to shut
ourselves off from it.

[12]. . . *training us to renounce irreligion and worldly passions, and to live sober, upright, and godly lives in this world,* . . .

The Apostle describes how God's grace revealed in Jesus Christ leads the Christian first of all in a negative fashion to make a radical break with the life of " irreligion and worldly passions." For Christian *baptism* puts an end to man's life of sin, when he clung to the wrongdoing and worldly pleasure (cf. 1 Jn. 2:16). " We were buried therefore with him by baptism into death, so that as Christ was raised from the dead by the glory of the Father, we too might walk in newness of life " (Rom. 6:4). And then God's grace continues the work of training up the plant whose roots took hold in baptism. He gives us strength for our new Christian life, which, in turn, is characterized in three respects. With regard to our own self, it is a life of prudence and sobriety; with regard to our fellow men, one of honesty; with regard to God, one of piety. No man can find strength in himself for such a life, but only in God's grace, which alone endows him with the force he needs. His awareness of being carried along by the power of this grace prompts the Apostle's boast: " I can do all things in him who strengthens me " (Phil. 4:13).

[13]. . . *awaiting our blessed hope, the appearing of the glory of our great God and Saviour Jesus Christ,* . . .

The Christian does not find life's final goal in this world; he is *waiting*; his life is built on hope in the second coming of the Lord. He perseveres in expectation of the coming fullness of salvation. This tenacious " steadfastness of hope in our Lord Jesus Christ " (1 Thess. 1:3), bound up with faith and love, is part of the foundation of any Christian life (cf. 1 Cor. 13:13). Christians must become ever more aware of " the hope to which he has called you " (Eph. 1:18). This hope is " a sure and steadfast anchor . . . that enters into the inner shrine behind the curtain " (Heb. 6:19), an anchor the Christian has cast deep into the sure ground of heaven.

The great day which awaits the Christian in " blessed hope " is the day when our great God and Saviour Jesus Christ returns from heaven in all the radiant splendor of his transfigured majesty, to lead his people into his kingdom: the *day of the second coming*. As he turns to contemplate the risen Lord's return in kingly power, the Apostle calls him not only " our Saviour," " our Redeemer," but also " the great God."

Paul refers continually in his letters to the fact that one of the main pillars of a Christian's life is hope. These words from the Epistle to the Hebrews: " Let us hold fast the confession of our hope without wavering " (Heb. 10:23) are surely very apt for us modern Christians too. For we very easily make ourselves nicely at home in this world, and easily forget that our true home is " in heaven," that is, in God (Phil. 3:20).

¹⁴ *. . . who gave himself for us to redeem us from all iniquity and to purify for himself a people of his own who are zealous for good deeds.*

Jesus Christ shows himself as Saviour in his readiness to die for all mankind: " God shows his love for us in that while we were yet sinners Christ died for us " (Rom. 5:8). He, the representative, gave his life in expiation for the whole human race fallen prey to death. " For the Son of man . . . came not to be served but to serve, and to give his life as a ransom for many " (Mk.

10:45). In this way Jesus Christ achieved his redemptive work, freeing us from " all iniquity," from the tyrannous power of sin which held us all in bondage.

Ransomed by Christ, Christians have become *his property,* God's people of the new covenant. Paul uses the words the Old Testament used of the Israelites, when he describes the Christians as the new and purified people of God. The Jews were God's own people, chosen in the covenant of his tender compassion, love, and faithfulness. The Christians are the holy church called in deep love by Christ to be his own, to be his holy and un-blemished bride " without spot or wrinkle or any such thing " (cf. Eph. 5:25–27). Freed from all sin and made pure and holy in Christ as his people, Christians must make visible in good works the great dignity of their vocation. Is it not right that precisely through the new life Christians have received in Christ, the world should come to feel and see that God's grace really offers salvation to all men? The world must realize that his grace alone is the fountainhead of strength for this new life.

Titus's Mission to Preach (2:15)

¹⁵*Declare these things; exhort and reprove with all authority. Let no one disregard you.*

Titus must preach this message of *God's grace,* revealed in Jesus Christ as the source of all strength for a Christian life. What a contrast this makes with those " empty talkers and deceivers " (1:10) who are " upsetting whole families by teaching for base gain " (1:11) the " Jewish myths " and " commands of men who reject the truth " (1:14). And Titus must undertake this task in a spirit of positive decision, not one of fear and apprehension.

The final warning, " Let no one disregard you," leads us to wonder if Titus, like Timothy, was still a young man at this time (cf. 2:7; I Tim. 4:12). If he was, he may have experienced difficulties in his position as leader of the church, for no one likes to be given directives or correction by the young, much less to be disciplined by them. And, too, it was usual for the Christian community to have older men at its head. On the other hand, is it that Titus was in some way clumsy and unskillful? We do not know enough about his life to be certain. In any case, in his letter, and especially at this point in it, Paul places himself with all his authority as " apostle of Jesus Christ " behind his disciple and deputy. He points out that the power of the Christian message is in no way lessened by the person who preaches it, or by his youth. Jesus himself had told his disciples: " He who hears you hears me, and he who rejects you rejects me, and he who rejects me rejects him who sent me " (Lk. 10:16).

Duties Towards the Authorities
and One's Fellow Men (3:1–2)

After the interruption dealing with God's grace as the fount of our strength, the Apostle takes up again the thread of his instructions for the various classes of Christians (cf. 2:1–10). He now lays down the duties they have to the authorities (3:1) and to their fellow men (3:2).

Submission to Authority (3:1)

[1]*Remind them to be submissive to rulers and authorities, to be obedient, to be ready for any honest work, . . .*

In his directive for ordering the Christian life, the Apostle finally turns his attention to the duties the young churches of Crete have towards the pagan authorities there. It is evident from his words " remind them to be submissive " that he had already dealt with the question in his earlier teaching and instruction. Maybe this is why he confines himself here to very brief remarks. He tells Titus to remind the Christians about their duties towards their rulers, duties which concern them all. As Christians they owe *submission and obedience* even to pagan authorities. He had laid down the relevant principles in his letter to the Romans: " Let every person be subject to the governing authorities. For there is no authority except from God, and those that exist have been instituted by God. Therefore he who resists the authorities resists what God has appointed, and those who resist will incur judgment " (Rom. 13:1-2). Paul, then, sees God himself as standing behind the power of the State, because he is the ultimate founder of human community; in the end, obedience to the State and its rulers is obedience to God. The Apostle is firm about this principle, even though Nero was Emperor at the time; and in the First Epistle to Timothy he calls for prayers for " kings and all who are in high positions " (1 Tim. 2:2). His demand for submission and obedience holds good even with respect to non-Christian authorities. This whole admonition is perhaps prompted by the frequent disturbances of the peace which we know to have been a feature of life on the island (cf. 1:2).

A second Christian duty is that of being *ready for any honest work*: work, that is, for the common good. This is, after all, no more than putting into practice the commandment to love one's neighbor, and this love must know no bounds and no restrictions; it must not even stop short at one's enemies (cf. Mt. 5:38-48).

Behavior Towards One's Fellow Men (3:2)

²*. . . to speak evil of no one, to avoid quarreling, to be gentle, and to show perfect courtesy towards all men.*

In the young churches of Crete the Christians live in the midst of a pagan population. However much this environment oppresses the individual Christian through slander, scorn, or personal offense, he must prove himself the disciple of Jesus Christ. He must always show patient forgiveness and self-sacrificing love; he must not repay injury with injury, but overcome evil with good (cf. Rom. 12:20f.). Paul's words to the church of Corinth about himself and his co-workers apply equally to the Christians of Crete: " When reviled, we bless; when persecuted, we endure; when slandered, we try to conciliate " (1 Cor. 4:12-13).

The Rebirth We Have Received (3:3-8)

Life Before Conversion (3:3)

³*For we ourselves were once foolish, disobedient, led astray, slaves to various passions and pleasures, passing our days in malice and envy, hated by men and hating one another; . . .*

In the preceding verse (3:2) the Apostle has demanded of the Christians patient forgiveness and self-sacrificing love for their pagan fellow citizens. This tolerant and forbearing attitude towards men from whom they suffer injustice of all sorts must stem from humble self-awareness: they must never forget that a short time ago they were no better than these men. Paul briefly sketches man's *unredeemed state* before conversion to Christ. As in many of his other letters, he describes contemporary pagan life from the standpoint of his experience and his knowledge of Jesus Christ; the contrast with the Christian life is, as always, very sharp. Although he was a member of the chosen people of Israel, he considers himself in this respect on a par with Cretans and with all mankind. Before their conversion the Christians were " foolish," with no understanding of God and godly things. " Since they did not see fit to acknowledge God, God gave them up to a base mind " (Rom. 1:28). Their mind was in darkness, and they were alienated from the life of God, because of the " ignorance that is in them, due to their hardness of heart " (Eph. 4:18). They were " disobedient," rebellious against God's will and his commands, and so they strayed ever farther from his truth into false ways. They had become slaves to their own desires; God had given them up to " dishonorable passions " (Rom. 1:26). They lived in the ways of the flesh, " following the desires of body and mind," and so " were by nature children of wrath, like the rest of mankind " (Eph. 2:3). Crass egoism ruled their life, manifesting itself in malice and envy. Strife, quarreling, and hatred for each other were the prominent features of their daily life. The Apostle, enlightened by the grace of Christ, can see the great and terrible darkness which lies like a pall over life unredeemed by Jesus Christ. This has been their past, and Christians must never forget it.

Salvation Through Rebirth (3:4–6)

  *. . . but when the goodness and loving kindness of God our Saviour appeared, *[5]*he saved us, not because of deeds done by us*

in righteousness, but in virtue of his own mercy, by the washing
of regeneration and renewal in the Holy Spirit, ⁶which he poured
out upon us richly through Jesus Christ our Saviour, . . .

The turning point in human history came at the moment
God had appointed in his plan for man's salvation. God's great
deed dawned in Christ's birth, and was achieved in his death on
the cross. His *goodness and loving kindness* appeared in Jesus
Christ, his incarnate son. These two attributes of God are per-
sonified in solemn words, in the courtly style of that time. A
light has appeared in our darkness: God's immeasurable
" goodness " in coming not as avenging judge to sinful man, but
as merciful friend; and his " loving kindness " in stooping down
in love to the men he has created, despite the absoluteness of the
distance which separates him from them. What a lofty picture
of God the Apostle gives us in these two words! And the
turning point in human history which dawned in the birth and
death of Jesus Christ brings a great turning point to the life of
each individual man.

If the Christian unites himself in true faith to Jesus Christ,
who is this goodness and loving kindness of God made man; if
he gives himself totally to Christ, God will save him from
eternal death. He will save him through the *washing of regener-*
ation, in the waters of baptism. The term " regeneration " was
taken over from contemporary hellenistic Judaism, and applied
to Christian baptism in which man was created anew: " the
old has passed away, behold, the new has come " (2 Cor. 5 : 17).
In baptism a new principle of supernatural life is planted in
man's soul, so that he begins to live on a new and higher plane.

To be baptized is to be born of God (Jn. 1 : 12f.), to be " born
from above " (Jn. 3 : 3), to be " born of water and the Spirit "

(Jn. 3:5). With the "washing of regeneration" goes the "renewal in the Holy Spirit, which he poured out upon us richly through Jesus Christ our Saviour." This gift of the Spirit fulfills the prophecy of Joel: "And it shall come to pass afterward, that I will pour out my spirit on all flesh" (Joel 2:28). So in baptism a man is made into a new being. Through God's gift of grace, his human nature with all its sinful desires is filled with fresh strength for life in the spirit. He is truly a "new creation" (2 Cor. 5:17).

The words *regeneration and renewal* imply that something has happened at man's deepest level: new life has been given, the old life has been transformed. His whole being has been raised by God's creative act to a new level of life. All that he needs has been given him. No deed of his own has any part in this new birth. The two words Paul uses rule this out, and stress once more one of the clearest fundamental concepts of the Apostle's preaching: that this salvation was brought about "not because of deeds done by us in righteousness, but in virtue of his own mercy." All human works and merit are quite ruled out: God's "mercy" alone has saved us. The "regeneration" we have received in baptism is the work of the Trinity, the Father, Son, and Holy Spirit; and in this rebirth we have been pardoned and raised up to live a new and higher life.

The Apostle calls on every Christian in these young churches to remember the great change which came about in their lives when they were baptized, a change each one of them had only recently experienced. We may well ask ourselves if we today have not in many ways let the full meaning of baptism fade out of our lives, or even entirely disappear. Can we say we are aware of what "regeneration and renewal in the Holy Spirit" really are, and what they really imply?

Christians Are Heirs to Eternal Life (3:7)

[7] . . . so that we might be justified by his grace and become heirs in hope of eternal life.

Again the Apostle underlines the same fundamental concept of his preaching: that no man is entitled to boast. For we are justified " by his grace "; we owe our new, supernatural life to his good favor and immeasurable love. Hence Paul's words apply to every Christian when he asks: " What have you that you did not receive? If then you received it, why do you boast as if it were not a gift?" (1 Cor. 4:7). And yet another gift the Christians receive in their rebirth to new life is that of being made *heirs to the eternal life* they hope for. In the " washing of regeneration and renewal in the Holy Spirit " they are accepted as children of God: " God has sent the Spirit of his Son into our hearts, crying, ' Abba! Father!' So through God you are . . . a son, and if a son then an heir " (Gal. 4:6–7). Christians do not yet possess the fullness of eternal life; that is the goal they hope to reach. And this unshakable hope bears them along through life. They have already been given the pledge of reaching the goal when they received the Holy Spirit in baptism. So they can await God's judgment with courage and confidence that it will liberate them finally to share in everlasting life.

They Are Obliged to Live a Christian Life (3:8)

[8]The saying is sure. I desire you to insist on these things, so that those who have believed in God may be careful to apply themselves to good deeds; these are excellent and profitable to men.

Again Paul emphasizes the truth of the teaching he has just expounded in 3:4-7. The phrase he uses is a formula common in the pastoral epistles. Then he demands that Titus act decisively in proclaiming and upholding the good news of God's saving work, especially in view of the activity of the false teachers in the church, the " empty talkers and deceivers " who are endangering the faith and " upsetting whole families by teaching . . . what they have no right to teach " (1:10). In his preaching of " regeneration and renewal in the Holy Spirit " Titus must bring home to his Christians, who are new to the faith, that to receive the gift of salvation is to incur at the same time a moral task and obligation. Living in the midst of a pagan world, they must preserve the new, divine life God has given them, and make it bear fruit effectively in a truly Christ-like way of life. True faith *has* to be like that (cf. Gal. 5:6). The saving gift received in baptism demands one's gratitude, and this will enable one to have the right sentiments towards one's fellows, and to lead a really active Christian life. Wherever this outlook prevails, and life is informed by these genuine Christian values, the community is in a sound and healthy state. But all the nonsense the false teachers spread abroad will do nothing to save mankind or to bring eternal life. The letter proper closes with yet another warning on this topic.

Another Warning Against the False Teachers (3:9-11)

Controversy and Dissension Must Be Renounced (3:9)

[9]*But avoid stupid controversies, genealogies, dissensions, and quarrels over the law, for they are unprofitable and futile.*

Like the first section of the letter, this second one also closes with remarks about the false teachers. Again, as in the other pastoral epistles, there are only brief references to their preaching. It is a question of "stupid controversies," fantastic discourses and speculations about genealogies, bickering and quarreling about the Old Testament law, and especially about the rules concerning food and ritual purity. The Apostle does not go more deeply into any of it. He has only the one clear and curt instruction: *avoid it*. And he gives his reason: it is unprofitable, futile, and harmful. This is in sharp contrast with the true Christian life marked out by good works; these are " excellent and profitable to men," and lead to eternal life. This brief command simply to reject the false teachings *en bloc* is characteristic of Paul's warnings to Timothy and Titus in the pastoral epistles. He never permits them to delve more deeply into the false doctrines. There is never any theological discussion of the ideas involved. This contrasts with the very different attitude the Apostle shows in other writings. In his Epistle to the Romans and Epistle to the Galatians, in several chapters of both letters to the Corinthians, in the First and Second Epistles to the Thessalonians, and also in those to the Ephesians and to the Colossians, he often indulges in prolonged and penetrating arguments about his opponents' errors. Is this because Timothy and Titus are not yet prepared for controversy of this sort? Or perhaps experience has taught Paul that there is no point now in such discussions, that to discuss is merely to present new dangers to the faith, which has now reached the stage of being taught as a normative tradition. And it is this tradition that is being so severely threatened in the newly founded churches of Crete.

Behavior Towards the False Teachers (3:10–11)

[10]*As for a man who is factious, after admonishing him once or twice, have nothing more to do with him,* [11]*knowing that such a person is perverted and sinful; he is self-condemned.*

Finally, the Apostle gives his deputy an important practical rule for dealing with the false teachers. They are a danger to the faith, and so have become a threat to the continued existence of the Christian communities. That is why Paul's demands are hard and unyielding. Titus is to correct the false teacher once or twice. In the Second Epistle to Timothy he tells him to correct his opponents " with gentleness. God may perhaps grant that they will repent and come to know the truth " (2 Tim. 2:25). So we can suppose that in these first warnings Titus also is to be gentle as well as firm.

Should we think of this process of admonition in terms of what is laid down in Matthew 18:15–16? If so, the first warning would take place in private, the second in the presence of one or two witnesses. In any case, if these warnings are fruitless and the false teacher persists in his disobedience, rejecting all advice and refusing to change his opinion, Titus must break off relations with him entirely. Paul's command here is very brusque: " Have nothing more to do with him." We may wonder if this means that the false teacher would, at a solemn church assembly, be banned from the community (cf. 1 Tim. 5:20; Mt. 18:17). Titus's discipline must be harsh when the *safety and preservation of the church's faith* is in question. For that is the costly treasure the Apostle has entrusted to him, and he must keep it pure and untainted, he must take care of it, and in his turn hand it down as a rich legacy. When this treasure is threatened by a false teacher, the only thing to do is to cut him off decisively. This is surely an echo of the hard words of Jesus: " And if your hand or your foot causes you to sin, pluck it out and throw it from you " (Mt. 18:8f.).

Titus, however, does not have to pass final judgment in such a case. He is to leave the false teacher to the judgment of his own innermost self. And the false teacher, if he sinfully persists in his activities after he has been warned, and remains obstinately disobedient against his better knowledge and his conscience, shows himself to be " perverted and sinful." His own conscience is his judge, and departure from the community of his brothers and sisters is the sentence it passes on him.

THE CLOSE OF THE LETTER
(3:12-15)

PERSONAL COMMISSIONS AND GREETINGS
(3:12–15)

Paul has dealt with the two questions which lay close to his heart: the ordering of the church's life on Crete (1:5-9; 2:1—3:7) and the problem of the false teachers (1:10-16; 3:8-11). Now, as in other letters, he adds a few personal notes: there are some missions to be undertaken (3:12-14) and greetings to be sent (3:15a), and he ends by giving his blessing (3:15b).

Personal Commissions (3 : 12–14)

¹²*When I send Artemas or Tychicus to you, do your best to come to me at Nicopolis, for I have decided to spend the winter there.*

Paul's first request concerns Titus himself. The Apostle is fairly soon going to send one of his fellow workers, either Artemas or Tychicus, to Crete to relieve Titus from his post and take over from him the leadership of the church on the island. We know nothing more about Artemas, but Tychicus is mentioned in the Acts of the Apostles as Paul's companion when he returned from Macedonia to Asia Minor at the end of his third missionary journey (Acts 20:4). He came from that part of the world (Acts 20:4), and it was he that delivered Paul's letters to the Colossians (Col. 4:7) and to the Ephesians (Eph. 6:21). He was to pass on to the Christians there his personal knowledge of the Apostle's condition in prison (Eph. 6:21f.; Col. 4:7-9). Paul evidently thought highly of him: he calls him his " beloved brother and faithful minister and fellow servant in the Lord " (Col. 4:7). In the Second Epistle to Timothy he reports that he has sent him to Ephesus (2 Tim. 4:12). Maybe this " faithful minister " had been not only Paul's co-worker but also, as many people think, his secretary.

Titus is himself asked to come quickly, when his successor arrives, to Nicopolis, where the Apostle is spending the winter. This was a town in Epirus, called " Nicopolis " in memory of Augustus's victory at the battle of Actium (31 BC). It had developed into a cultural center of Hellenic life. We may wonder if Paul's choice of this town on the Adriatic means that he intended further journeys in the west.

Titus, then, is soon going to leave the Christian communities of Crete. But despite this forthcoming change he must discharge his apostolic ministry with all his energies right up to the last moment. Even now, when he knows he will be relieved of his duties, he must continue to " teach what befits sound doctrine " (2:1), show himself " a model of good deeds " (2:7), and " exhort and reprove with all authority " (2:15), bearing powerful witness to the good news of Jesus Christ. He must perform his duties faithfully until he leaves, for " it is required of stewards that they be found trustworthy," and he is one of the " servants of Christ and stewards of the mysteries of God " (1 Cor. 4:1f.).

[13]*Do your best to speed Zenas the lawyer and Apollos on their way; see that they lack nothing.* [14]*And let our people learn to*

*apply themselves to good deeds, so as to help cases of urgent
need, and not to be unfruitful.*

A second task Titus has is to look after Zenas and Apollos.
These two men probably brought Paul's letter over to Crete and
were going on from there perhaps to Alexandria, which was
Apollos's home town (Acts 18:24). Zenas is unknown to us from
any other New Testament source. Maybe he is called " the
lawyer " because he had previously studied the Jewish law, or
maybe because he was a practicing Roman lawyer. Apollos,
however, is well known from his activity in Ephesus (Acts
18:24–26) and Corinth; he was a Jewish Christian, had studied
philosophy, and was a gifted speaker. Titus must take all possible care to ensure that these two Christian teachers "lack
nothing " in the way of provisions and equipment for their
journey. He must mobilize the forces of the Christian community on their behalf. It would be wrong for the Cretan
Christians to fall behind the Jews and pagans in their willingness to put themselves out for their traveling teachers. This is
an opportunity for them to prove their love by joining in to help
wherever help is called for. Practical concern of this sort must
be the fruit of their true Christian life.

It is noticeable that *good works* are greatly stressed in the
pastoral epistles. Titus is called on to train the young churches
in practical love and help. This is, of course, not to say that
Paul neglects the importance of " good works " (which have
nothing to do with justification by works) in his earlier letters.
The particularly strong emphasis in the pastoral epistles is due to
their practical purpose. " Good works " are to be the evidence
that Christians have really received an effective, powerful principle of new life (cf. 2 Tim. 3:17). God's saving and strengthen-

ing grace must become visible in a Christian's daily life. True faith brings concern for others, and real action (Gal. 5:6).

Greetings and Final Blessing (3:15)

¹⁵*All who are with me send greetings to you. Greet those who love us in the faith. Grace be with you all.*

Paul's greetings at the end of this letter are very brief. His companions greet Titus and the Cretan churches, but their names are not mentioned as they often are in other letters. Titus must pass their good wishes on to all his Christian people, who are bound to the Apostle through the bond of faith and love. They all belong to the one family of the Lord Jesus Christ; the same bond of brotherhood in faith and love embraces all of them, for " you have one teacher, and you are all brethren " (Mt. 23:8).

The final blessing, written in Paul's own hand, is meant equally for Titus and for all the Cretan Christians. It is evident how much he had these newly founded communities in mind as he wrote. He is deeply concerned for them, that they hold fast to the faith entrusted to them, that they prove themselves by a true Christian life, and that they do not fall victim to the subversive work of the false teachers. They too, then, as well as Titus, are included in the Apostle's final blessing.

He wishes them all that Christians could wish each other: " grace," the grace of God in which we are saved, the grace whose boundless riches " coming ages " will reveal (cf. Eph. 2:5-7).

The Epistle to Philemon

INTRODUCTION

Reception into the Church

Opposition and Anxiety

The shortest of all St. Paul's epistles has often been described as a note. However, this is not perfectly accurate, as it deals with a problem which the Church always had to contend with.

When St. Paul sent the fugitive slave Onesimus back to his master Philemon, after he had been converted and had received baptism, he expressed the wish that he should welcome him lovingly, as a brother. In making this request he had to be prepared for a certain amount of opposition. Was the slave's flight to go unpunished? Was he not responsible for losses which should be made good? He had disturbed the social order of things and his example was sure to become a model for others. What would people think of Christianity? His conversion might be only a pose which he adopted to escape the consequences of his crime.

Preparation of Heart

St. Paul prepares Philemon and the church which assembled in his house to welcome back the fugitive slave who had now been converted. Most probably, the Christian community would share the reluctance and anxiety of the master of the house who was their host. St. Paul had overcome the strenuous opposition of

55

those who clung to the law and called themselves clean, in order to bring the gentiles into the Church; this brief letter was the principal means he used now, in order to prepare the hearts of his readers and overcome their opposition to his request. We do not know to what extent he succeeded, but no one could resist this most delightful of all his letters. How could all those who are anxious to find their way to unity in Christ be incorporated into the Church, if the Church and all its members are not constantly prepared anew to welcome those who were separated and are now anxious to return or seek to be admitted to the Church? Graciousness (*charis*) and affectionateness are the hallmarks of this "charming" letter of St. Paul. All those whose lives are spent as members of the Church must be animated by St. Paul's spirit, the spirit in which he prepared the church in Philemon's house to welcome back Onesimus.

Law and Love

Anxiety to restore due order must not prevent anyone who wants to be received into the Church from being given a warm welcome. It is St. Paul's wish that the converted slave should return to his master and he acknowledges that his master has a right to compensation; he wants all the demands of the law to be met. In the whole letter, we must remember that slavery is taken for granted as a permanent institution. The norms of the law held good for Christians too, just like all the other laws of the state in which they found themselves. As a man of his time, even St. Paul accepted this arrangement; he made no effort to come to terms with it in principle. His thoughts are on a completely different plane; he realizes, and he makes this clear precisely in this letter, that the new life in Christ has completely changed the differences which existed in human society. Christians are all members of the same body; they are brothers and sisters in Christ. Once it was put into practice in daily life, this line of thought was bound to lead inevitably to the abolition of slavery as an unworthy state of affairs; it was bound to lead to all men being treated as equals not only in matters of faith but in " civil life " also. The noblest forces of Christianity and paganism cooperated to attain this goal.

The point which St. Paul wishes to make here is this; when the old self has been put off and replaced by the new self which is created in God's image, all racial, social, and religious distinctions lose their meaning for those who have faith and before God. It makes no difference whether a person was formerly a Jew or a gentile or a " barbarian " (even one of the most uncivilized barbarians, a Scythian); it makes no difference whether he was a slave or a free man; once he has been incorporated into Christ by faith and baptism, he has received new life. A person's ordinary life, his national, cultural, and social heritage are obviously not affected by the rebirth which takes place at baptism; however, these natural values no longer play a decisive part. It is being in Christ that matters; Christ is all in all (Col. 3 : 4).

This new life gives rise to a reappraisal of moral values. A person who is in Christ must live by Christ; his brothers who share the same faith must acknowledge him as one in whom Christ lives. Behind this new appraisal stand Jesus' redeeming death and the application of this redemption to each individual by baptism which is received in faith.

For St. Paul, life in Christ and through Christ is not merely a matter of profound speculation or an exercise of thought which is completely divorced from the world; it is something which gives rise to moral duties in the problems of daily life. What God achieves in men through Christ gives rise to an obligation to lead a morally good life.

In his approach to Philemon, St. Paul himself gives pride of place to charity rather than strict justice. Although he is an apostle, he does not command him; instead, he asks him. He makes no demands on him, and leaves it to his own conscience to decide what is to be done. He is more anxious to encourage him to make progress in goodness than to lord it over him.

The Basis on which the Church Is Built Up

The reception of a person who was a stranger to the Church into the Christian community serves to build up the Church. A new member is incorporated into it, and so the Church is built up. But the Church is also subject to an interior process of building up; a new member can be incorporated only if faith and love are fully developed in the Church.

A new member can be accepted by the other members into the unity of one body, only if they regard him in a spirit of faith as their brother, as a new creature, as someone who has been brought to birth by the gospel and is in Christ. It is the love which springs from a lively faith which really accomplishes the incorporation of the new member. " Taking our stand on the truth, we are anxious to grow up to his stature in all things, in love; he, Christ, is the head. By his influence, the whole body is organized and held together by the bond of what each single part contributes according to its ability. In this way, the body reaches its full growth, building itself up in love " (Eph. 4:15).

The Church is made up of " Christ and all the saints " (v. 5); it is a community in which everyone shares everything in common. All the members of the Church are brothers; they " share " in each other's being. At a time when the Church is on the way to becoming the Church of the nations and of all men, when every single Christian is called upon to incorporate all men and all things into Christ, and free himself from all social, national, racial, religious, and cultural prejudices, so that Christ may be all in all—at such a time the short epistle to Philemon has a great mission. In our concern for individual human beings, it is not merely noble ideas which will be decisive; it is the manner in which these ideas are incarnated by living persons and presented to the world.

The Epistle to Philemon is a masterpiece of pastoral writing. Everything which might separate Christians is bridged " in Christ "; everything which was far away has been brought near, in the eyes of faith; the chasms between men are surmounted by the fact that they are brothers. The harsh claims of justice are tempered by love; all feeling of superiority is dispelled by the willingness to serve which love demands.

Always Lovable

A Christian's manner of speaking must be " always gracious [*charis*] and seasoned with salt " (Col. 4:6). The Epistle to Philemon meets these requirements to perfection. It is a "miracle of tact and fine feeling."

St. Paul cast his plea for the fugitive slave in a form which is half prose, half hymn. The Epistle to the Ephesians, which was written almost at the same time, is also artistically composed. His style is ritual, ceremonious, liturgical. The Epistle to Philemon is a gracious, delightful, and charming composition. He employs unusual expressions taken from ritual language, together with words from the world of business, law, and the philosophical schools. He could only have made out a promissory note to make Philemon's losses good with a good-humored laugh. He did it with all the essential legal formalities, although he knew well that he had nothing and never could have anything with which he could redeem it.

A person who wishes to prevail by means of love must discover the way in which to show his love. It is not enough for a Christian that he should have love in his heart; he must show it in his words and in his attitude, in the lovableness of his whole being. The Epistle to Philemon is a picture-book which serves to illustrate the New Testament hymn of charity (1 Cor. 13).

OUTLINE

THE OPENING OF THE LETTER
(vv. 1-3)

INTRODUCTORY VERSES (vv. 1–3)

In the introductory verses of his letter, St. Paul employs a formula which was used in public and official documents in the Greek world. Even the shortest and most "private" of all his letters follows the pattern of the great epistles he wrote to the churches and the same schema. St. Paul wrote his letter to Philemon as an "apostolic letter," which should be of importance for the Church in all ages.

The author of the letter and the recipient are named in the first sentence (vv. 1–2), while the second contains St. Paul's good wishes (v. 3).

¹Paul, the prisoner of Jesus Christ, and the brother Timothy, to Philemon our well beloved fellow laborer ²and the sister Appia, to our fellow soldier Archippus, and the church in your house.

Apostle and Witness (v. 1a)

The apostolic pair, Paul and Timothy, are the senders of the letter. They are "brothers" in office and they present themselves as authorized witnesses. Two witnesses whose testimony is in agreement constitute a valid proof (cf. Deut. 19 : 15). The message they send in the letter is intended to have binding force and be convincing; it is meant to crush any opposition which might be aroused against it.

St. Paul writes as a prisoner of Jesus Christ. He used this

title, not in order to arouse sympathy and so prepare the way for his request and his exhortation, but in order to remind Philemon of Christ who stands before him in the person of his imprisoned apostle. He writes as Christ's martyr and apostle; it is as such that he claims a hearing.

The chains which he wears are Christ's chains. It is Christ who allows his apostle to share his own chains. It is to him that St. Paul dedicates all his thoughts and all his service; Christ lives in him. The chains he wears are " Christ's scars " (Gal. 6:17), which St. Paul bears in his own body. He carries about continually in his body the dying state of Jesus, so that the living power of Jesus may be manifested in his body too (2 Cor. 4:10). It is in suffering that his apostolic labors reach their highest peak; he suffers so that grace made manifold in many lives may increase the sum of gratitude which is offered to God's glory (2 Cor. 4:15).

The Community (vv. 1b–2)

The letter is addressed to Philemon and his wife Appia, together with Archippus, the superior of the Christian community, and the community which met in Philemon's house. Philemon owned a house at Colossae which was on the great trade route leading from Ephesus through the tortuous valleys of the Meander and the Lycus to Apameia and thence to Tarsus, via the Cilician Gates. The town most probably shared in the wool industry of the Lycus valley. Philemon had been converted by St. Paul (v. 19), probably during the time he was ministering at Ephesus (AD 54–57).

The community which assembled at Philemon's house to cele-
brate the liturgy was a part of the church at Colossae; other
members of the church assembled in other houses. Even in
Jerusalem, in the early days, the Christians used to break bread
" in this house or that " (Acts 2 : 46). St. Paul mentions similar
household churches at Corinth and Rome, in Aquila and
Prisca's home (1 Cor. 16 : 19; Rom. 16 : 5), and at Laodicea in
Nymphas's home (Col. 4 : 15). These cells were united under an
authorized superior who " shared St. Paul's battle " to form the
church in each city. The " Lord's Supper " could be celebrated
in the small groups formed by these household communities,
while the brother and sister relationships which exist between
Christians could be fostered and experienced. There, too,
Christ's word could be assimilated in a more personal fashion.

The church in Philemon's house was an organized community and Philemon and Appia put their home at its disposal.
They are given particular mention among the other Christians
because they are benefactors of the community and its
" patrons." Next the head of the community is named, while the
community as a whole is mentioned last. The Church's organization is not based solely on legal norms; it depends also on the
" order " of practical charity and gratitude. The Church
acknowledges the charity shown it by giving its benefactors a
place of honor even at the liturgical celebration.

The letter concerned Philemon alone primarily, but St. Paul
does not address it only to him; he addresses it solemnly and
officially to the community of which Philemon was a member.
He makes known his wish, not in private, but before the whole
Church. What passes between one Christian and another affects
the church which is assembled in a particular place and, through
it, it affects the Church at large. The community gathered

in Philemon's house represents the universal Church. Every Christian bears responsibility for the Church.

Philemon is called well beloved because he is a Christian. God has bestowed his love on Christians (Rom. 8:28, 31-39), and chosen them out in his love (Eph. 1:4f.); he has poured out his love in their hearts (Rom. 5:5). In return, he demands that they should be guided by love. When a person appeals to a Christian's love, he should never be disillusioned.

St. Paul introduces Philemon as one who " shares his labors "; he is on the same level as Mark and Luke (v. 24), Prisca and Aquila (Rom. 16:3), Epaphroditus (Phil. 2:25) and Clement (Phil. 4:3). Every Christian shares St. Paul's labors, because he labors in the service of God's kingdom which is to come and is anxious for the spread of the gospel; for its sake, he undertakes any toil (1 Thess. 3:2; Col. 4:11).

St. Paul calls Appia his sister. " Well beloved " and " brother " (sister) are corresponding ideas (v. 16; 1 Thess. 2:8). Love finds its expression in the fact that Christians treat one another as brothers and sisters. A real Christian is a person who is guided by love (*agape*) and realizes that all other Christians are his brothers and sisters. He lives by this conviction and shares the work of proclaiming the gospel.

Archippus is described as " a fellow soldier " with St. Paul (Phil. 2:25). In the church at Colossae, he had fulfilled the task which was committed to him in the Lord's service (Col. 4:17). He held office in the church there and was, most likely, its superior. St. Paul's own labors and sharing in them take the form of fighting a battle (Phil. 4:3; 2 Cor. 10:4). It is a struggle against the princedoms and powers, against those who have mastery of the world in these dark days, against malign influences in an order higher than ours (Eph. 6:12).

Good Wishes (v. 3)

St. Paul is not content with a formula of good wishes; instead, he gives them a blessing. The formula is composed of three elements and this, together with its resemblance to the Jewish form of blessing, indicates that it was intended for liturgical use. Even this " private " letter was intended to be read out at the celebration of the liturgy.

³Grace be yours and peace from God our Father and our Lord Jesus Christ.

Grace and peace mean the salvation which God has given us through Christ. Jewish letter-writers wished their correspondents peace, meaning well-being; Christ's apostle adds to peace the word grace. Grace and peace are the saving gifts which God has bestowed on us in his love and kindness. " We are at peace with God, through our Lord Jesus Christ, through whom we have access, by faith, to the salvation which we enjoy " (Rom. 5: 1f.).

God, our Father, is the source of our redemption, but the Lord Jesus Christ is the Mediator who brings it to us. This phrase, which rounds off St. Paul's blessing, is a Christian's profession of faith, " Jesus Christ is the Lord " (Phil. 2: 11). Anyone who professes this faith and, through faith in the Lord Jesus Christ, has God for his Father, obtains salvation.

THE BODY OF THE LETTER
(vv. 4–24)

INTRODUCTORY THANKSGIVING:
BUILDING UP THE CHURCH (vv. 4–7)

The introductory thanksgiving (*eucharistia*) of the Epistle to Philemon is a hymn of thanks which can be divided into an introduction followed by three couplets. St. Paul offers these thanks for the progress the church in Philemon's house has made.

The first couplet mentions faith and love, which are the spiritual foundations of the Church. Love takes pride of place. The second couplet is centered on the thought that love must be active. It must find its expression in good actions; it is only in this way that it can be a light to the unbelievers. The first line of the third couplet ends with the words "in your love," while the second ends with "by you, brother." The new life which the faithful share, the fact that they enjoy redemption, is expressed principally in brotherly love.

The three couplets give us an outline of the Christian in his relation to Christ and his fellow Christians. The closing phrase of each couplet mentions this. The first closes with the words "the Lord Jesus and all the saints," both of whom taken together make up the new people of God. The second ends with the words (literally) "up to Christ Jesus." The Church must grow up to a due proportion with Christ (Eph. 4:15f.). The last couplet ends on the word "brother." The members of the Church are brothers who are united with one another in love. The Church is the community of brothers who are gathered around the Lord Jesus as the new people of God.

These verses contain a beautiful picture of the interior and exterior building up of the Church. God himself lays the foundations, faith and love (first couplet). It is faith and love together which lead to action, to the mutual sharing of what each one has, to " good actions in the faith " (second couplet). The harvest which this living faith and active love produce is happiness, consolation, encouragement. In

73

this way, the Church is built up on the foundation which God laid, until it reaches "perfect manhood, that maturity which is proportioned to the full stature of Christ " (Eph. 4:13).

Grateful Remembrance (v. 4)

Even in his prayers, St. Paul remains an apostle and a pastor. He never forgets those whom he had converted and his recollection of them takes the form of thanksgiving.

⁴I give thanks to my God, as I always remember you in my prayers. . . .

Praising God and thanking him are the basic acts of the adoration which we owe God and of the virtue of religion (Rom. 1:21). The purpose of all apostolic labor is that more and more people should be filled with gratitude, to God's glory (2 Cor. 4:15). A Christian must give proof of abundant gratitude (Col. 2:7), because God's grace too is abundant. " I give thanks to my God " is an echo of the piety found in the psalms. The psalms are old vessels which are here filled with new content. God has become "my God " through Christ and the overflowing love which he brought.

Love and Faith (v. 5)

" Faith in Jesus Christ " and " love for all the saints " (Col. 1:4) are the foundations of the Christian life. St. Paul takes his cue from the science of rhetoric and connects the beginning of the sentence with the end (" love towards all the saints "), as well as bringing the two central elements together (" faith towards the Lord "). This also provides him with an effective ending for his sentence, " the Lord Jesus and all the saints."

⁵. . . *because I hear of your love and your faith in the Lord Jesus and for all the saints.*

Love and faith are gifts from God; they call for gratitude. Faith in Jesus of Nazareth as the Lord contains the root of all salvation, but this faith must find its expression in love. Such love proves itself by the practice of brotherly love, by showing love towards all the saints. Love is given pride of place, because a life which is guided by faith is primarily a life of love.

The saints are the Christians. God has called them out from the rest of mankind and incorporated them into his chosen people by baptism. They have now been cleansed from their sins and made new creatures, as a result of receiving the Spirit. They are saints and they are bound to show themselves saints in their daily lives (1 Thess. 4:3f.).

The Lord Jesus and all the saints belong together, just like Yahweh, the Lord, and Israel, his chosen people whom he sanctified. A Christian is incorporated into the holy people of the Lord Jesus by faith and love which sum up the whole law (Gal. 5:13f.). In this way, a person becomes a living Christian.

Good Actions in the Faith (v. 6)

St. Paul prays that the Church may grow, interiorly and exteriorly; his words show us how the Church is built up.

⁶I pray that the good you do in a spirit of faith may be effective in [promoting] the knowledge of all that is good among you until you grow up to Christ.

Faith finds its expression in love and love regards everything it has as the common property of all; it shows itself by sharing. Sharing is a form of doing good. " The whole community of believers had one heart and one soul; no one called anything he possessed his own; they held everything in common " (Acts 4:32).

The good actions which are inspired by faith serve to build up the Church. They prompt the unbelievers to recognize all the good which is to be found in Christians. Recognition of such goodness and wonder at it is one of the ways to faith in Christ. Love which is active exercises a missionary influence.

As a result of such good actions, performed in faith, the Church grows up to Christ. That is, it becomes more and more like Christ, it becomes proportionate to the completed growth of Christ (Eph. 4:13).

A Happiness and a Comfort (v. 7)

The interior growth of the Church is another enrichment for which St. Paul gives thanks.

⁷I find great happiness and comfort in your love; the hearts of the saints have been cheered by you, brother.

Brotherly love brings interior comfort to the Church, to St. Paul and the other Christians. It brings them happiness and comfort.

By means of these three blessings, the salvation which is promised for the end of time reaches into our world today. " The kingdom of God means rightness of heart, finding our peace and our joy in the Holy Spirit " (Rom. 14:17; cf. 15:13). Our Lord Jesus Christ and God, our Father, have shown us their love and given us unfailing comfort and welcome hope through his grace (1 Thess. 2:16). Refreshment is one of Christ's saving gifts (Mt. 11:26) and those who have been chosen out by God enjoy it (Acts 14:13). The brotherly love which characterizes the Church gives us a foretaste of eternal salvation; it builds up the Church, both interiorly and exteriorly.

"IN CHRIST" (vv. 8–20)

Philemon's slave, Onesimus, had run away from him and escaped to Rome; he would have no difficulty losing himself in the bustle of the imperial city. St. Paul was a prisoner in Rome at the time, but how or why Onesimus came into contact with him is a mystery. He won him over to Christianity (v. 10) and could have used his services (v. 11). However, he was reluctant to detain him without knowing his master's wishes. Therefore, he sent him back to his master in the company of his fellow worker, Tychicus (Col. 4:9), together with a letter of recommendation, the Epistle to Philemon.

The principal part of the letter is made up of five " strophes," each of which is artistically constructed. St. Paul chooses his words carefully, and the extraordinary plays on words (vv. 11:20), daring imagery, and the use of equivocal terms, together with the brilliance of his style and his finely balanced rhythm show that he intends to leave nothing undone in his efforts to achieve his purpose.

As an apostle, St. Paul enjoyed authority, but he approaches Philemon as a man making a request (vv. 8–9); he intercedes for Onesimus, his fugitive slave, who was now related to St. Paul and to his master in a different way, as a result of his baptism (vv. 10–12). St. Paul could have invoked the rights he had acquired over the converted slave, but he renounces his right (vv. 13–14). By baptism, Onesimus has become Paul's brother and Philemon's (vv. 15–16). In him it is St. Paul himself who comes (vv. 17–20).

A Request, Not a Command (vv. 8–9)

The " strophe " is constructed according to the schema a-b-a. St. Paul writes in the full consciousness of his apostolic authority to prescribe a duty (a); however, he raises his request to the level of love and begs a favor, instead of giving a command (b); but he begs this favor as an apostle and a martyr (a).

⁸For this reason, although I would have full authority in Christ to command you to do what is expected of you, ⁹I prefer rather to appeal to you by your charity, I, Paul, an ambassador, but at the moment a prisoner of Christ.

St. Paul would have been within his rights in commanding Philemon to give his runaway slave a loving welcome, now that he had been baptized. He was entitled to speak out in Christ; he possessed power and authority which Christ had given him to govern the Church. Moreover, he was speaking here of something which was a matter of " duty "; it concerned the ethical life of a Christian and implied a moral obligation (Eph. 5:4). The rulers of the Church hold their authority from Christ and they are entitled to speak to the faithful " somewhat freely," provided that it is a question of faith or morals. The Church is not based on a bond of love alone; it is also founded on authority and obedience. It is a " Church of law " as well as a " Church of charity."

Even though he has authority to command, St. Paul prefers to use friendly persuasion. This is half way between giving a person an admonition and making a request. He appeals to his love, not to obedience. Law is necessary, but it is love which must decide. A Christian who had no love would be nothing (cf. 1 Cor. 13:1-3). The human heart opens more easily to friendly persuasion than to a harsh command. What use would a command be in this case? It was a question of incorporating a person lovingly into a community of love, a person who according

to the ideas of the time had gone astray. Only friendly persuasion and an appeal to love will arouse love.

St. Paul makes his request as a *presbytes*. There is a play on
the word here, as it can mean either "an old man" or "an
ambassador." As an apostle, St. Paul is Christ's ambassador,
but it is also true that he was an old man when he wrote
the Epistle to Philemon. He also presents himself as a prisoner
of Christ, who was imprisoned for Christ's suffering on behalf
of his Church (Col. 1:24). He appears before Philemon as an
apostle and a martyr, but also as an old man and a prisoner.
It is as an old man and a prisoner that he introduces himself
primarily, and only then as an apostle who has power to command. The human aspect is to the fore, while his divine
authority remains in the background. His authority to command
is veiled under the form of a helpless petitioner, his power under
his powerlessness, his right to rule under his will to serve. The
ruler of the Church presents himself first as an ordinary human
being, before invoking his authority. The work of our salvation is accomplished with all the kindness and condescension
of the love of the God of infinite majesty (Tit. 3:4).

My Child (vv. 10–12)

St. Paul now makes known his request; he is appealing on behalf
of Onesimus, Philemon's runaway slave. Only he is not that
any more. In a "strophe" which is constructed on the same model
as the preceding one (a-b-a), St. Paul explains what he has
become, for him personally and for Philemon. Baptism causes
a complete change of values in human relationships. This is
demonstrated by the change in the meaning of the name
Onesimus, which is mentioned in the middle of the strophe.

¹⁰I appeal to you for my child, to whom I gave life while in chains, ¹¹Onesimus, who was once useless to you, but is now useful both to you and to me. ¹²I am sending him to you, that is, [I am sending] my own heart.

St. Paul calls Onesimus his child; he was his convert. Conversion to the faith by means of the gospel means bringing a person forth to new life. Onesimus is a child of sorrow, as he was begotten at a time when St. Paul was a prisoner and bore a martyr's witness. His rebirth to new life has its origin in Christ's teaching and propitiatory death, and in St. Paul's preaching and the suffering which the gospel caused him (Phil. 2:17), in faith and baptism.

There is a great difference between what Onesimus was once and what he is now. Baptism divides a Christian's life into two completely distinct periods; once a slave of sin, now a free man; once under sentence of death, now marked out for life; once the prey of sin and immorality, now holy and ashamed of his former behavior.

This is made even more clear by the beautiful play on words which St. Paul uses. However, this must be taken at its face value; it would be a mistake to press it too closely and conclude, for example, that St. Paul regarded Onesimus as a human being and a slave as being "useless." The subtle humor with which St. Paul describes the change which has taken place can only be appreciated by hearing the Greek words he uses; once a "useless" (*achrestos*) person, Onesimus ("Useful") has become, through Christ (*chrestos*), a "very useful" (*euchrestos*) person. By faith in Christ and baptism, he has become a member of Christ's body; in this way, he became "useful" to all the other members of the body in a completely new sense (1 Cor. 12:20–

27). Previously, he was of no interest to Christ or Christianity; now, his old name (Useful) enjoys new significance in Christ. This will be demonstrated by the very fact that the community gives him a loving welcome; so he will prove his " usefulness " by increasing their faith and the Christian magnanimity of his master.

After his conversion, St. Paul calls Onesimus his heart. He took him into his love (Phil. 17), so that he loved him as his own heart, as his own self, the very depths of his being. Converting a man taxes the strength of one's heart and all one's powers of conviction, together with the love of one's whole soul. If, like St. Paul, a person can say to a man, My heart, whom I love, my child to whom I have given my affection, in whom I have submerged myself, he can be sure that he has acted according to the mind of Christ. He will be prepared for the exercise of devoted love.

The law prescribed that fugitive slaves must be returned to their masters. Anyone who kept a fugitive slave for himself became guilty of an offense in private law as an accomplice. St. Paul, therefore, sends Onesimus back to his master; he uses the legal term when speaking of his decision to return him. But he sends him back as his heart, as a part of himself. All his compassion, all his sympathy go with him. Love respects the law, even if this imposes a strain on its own compassionate heart. "Charity does not claim its rights" (1 Cor. 13:5).

The runaway slave must stand before his master, but his father, Paul, will accompany him, for his heart goes with him and begs for mercy. Ultimately, it is Christ who accompanies him; Onesimus is in him and he has espoused his cause. No matter what a person may have made of himself, once he repents the church intercedes for him; Christ himself espouses his cause. Like St. Paul, Christ says of him, He is my heart. In his turn, such a man is entitled to say, "If God is for us, who is against us? He did not spare his own Son, but gave him up for us all; how could he fail to give us everything else together with him? Who can lay a charge against those whom God has chosen?" (Rom. 8:31–33).

An Act of Charity, Not a Legal Claim (vv. 13–14)

St. Paul could have laid claim to Onesimus's services by right. However, he is reluctant to detain him without the consent of his master. Philemon's good deed should be performed of his own free decision. In the strophe, which is made up of three verses (a–b–a), his "leave" is given a central place. St. Paul's appeal is addressed to man's most noble quality, his power of free decision.

[13]*I wanted to keep him here by me, to serve me in your place, [while I am] in chains for the gospel;* [14]*but I would not do anything without your leave, so that your good deed should not be the result of compulsion, but of a free decision.*

Those who preach the gospel have a right to the services of those whom they have converted by means of the gospel (Phil. 2:30; 1 Cor. 9:13ff.). This service is not due to the preacher or apostle, but to the gospel. Together with St. Paul, Timothy had served the gospel, like a son helping his father (Phil. 2:22). The gospel is something which all those are bound to serve who have experienced its power.

A person who has found his way into the Church and become

a servant of the gospel performs a service on behalf of everyone else who lives in the Church. He takes upon himself some of the worry and responsibility involved in the service of God's word as a deputy for others.

This willingness to serve the gospel is all the more imperative if the "preacher who has the duty to preach" the gospel is a prisoner. The fact that the gospel is imprisoned means that every available resource of strength must be called upon to help its course.

St. Paul renounces his right in Philemon's favor, so that he may have the opportunity of doing a good deed. Moral goodness is not achieved by force of command; it must be the result of a free choice inspired by love. Good should be done, not under compulsion, with regret, but of one's own free will. It is the cheerful giver God loves (2 Cor. 9:7).

It is not the direct approach by way of commands and duties which can be enforced that is better; the roundabout way of convincing and good-natured persuasion is more effective. This way, a person can be induced to make his own free choice, and this is the way God approached us. When Christ came to proclaim God's kingdom, he did not appear clothed in power; he appeared in the form of a helpless child and the powerlessness of death. The graciousness of our Lord Jesus Christ is revealed in the fact that he impoverished himself for our sakes, when he was so rich, so that we might become rich through his poverty (2 Cor. 8:9). Even the threats which are contained in the gospel presuppose faith, if they are to be efficacious, but faith is not something which can be forced; it is a free choice. God's saving activity is addressed to men who make a personal choice in love, for God's glory.

Our Brother (vv. 15–16)

Onesimus returns, not as Philemon's slave any more, but as his brother; he is his brother in Christ, for ever. Once more, the most important idea is in the center of the three line "strophe" (a–b–a). If Philemon remembers this, he cannot fail to give him a loving welcome.

St. Paul does nothing to undermine the powers and authorities responsible for order in the world; however, he makes it clear that as a result of baptism a slave enjoys a new position in relation to his master. The mutual relationship of slave and master is now determined, and consequently surmounted, by the facts of the redemption which Christ has brought. Similarly, in the Old Testament, the prophets did not correct abuses in society by political or social reforms; they corrected them by preaching a return to God and obedience to his will. When Christianity gained complete control of the ancient world, slavery as a social institution disappeared in practice and eventually in theory and legislation.

15For he was probably taken from you for a time, so that you might have him with you for eternity, not as a slave any more, but as far more than a slave—as a well loved brother, 16very [beloved], indeed, to me, but even more so to you on a human level and in the Lord.

When Onesimus ran away, it was by God's providential design. It was a loss, not a permanent flight. God ordained this loss to his eternal salvation. Faith takes more account of the dispositions of God's providence than of man's decisions, without denying man's free will.

Everything that God does has a purpose. St. Paul does not dare to decide infallibly what was the purpose of Onesimus's flight in God's providential design; "he was probably taken from you . . ." God's judgments are inscrutable (1 Cor. 2:16; Rom. 11:33f.). What men may think about the designs of his providence can be expressed only by way of conjecture. "We know that everything works together for the good of those who love God, those who are called according to his plan" (Rom. 8:28).

The loss resulted in Philemon's recovering his slave once more, in such a way that he is bound to "write off" his recovery; there are no further claims outstanding. They were separated only for a short time and God ordained that this should result in their being united for ever. God's providence is exercised in wisdom and overflowing love. Even though its first effect may result in loss, it eventually brings abundance.

Onesimus does not return as a slave, although it is true that he is still a slave as he comes back, and he remains such even after baptism. Conversion and baptism do not affect a person's social status. A poor person remains poor, even after baptism; a person who is of low birth is still of low birth when he is baptized; a person who had no education will still be ignorant in worldly matters, after he has received baptism (1 Cor. 1:26; 7:18–24). The salvation which we attain by faith and baptism does not improve one's earthly position.

As a result of baptism, however, a new "social" relationship has been added to the relationship between a slave and his master. The slave has become a well loved brother. It is this new aspect which counts most of all. "It does not matter any more whether a person is a Jew or a Greek, a slave or a freeman, a man or a woman. You have all become one in Christ Jesus"

(Gal. 3:28). This new dignity outshines the excellence the master once enjoyed over his slave.

Philemon has even more reason than St. Paul to regard Onesimus as a well loved brother; both on a natural level and in Christ. Onesimus is his brother, both in the natural order and in the new existence which Christ has given him. He is his brother in the natural order because he is bound to his master in a special way, according to the norms of society at the time. He is his brother in the Lord, because, like Philemon, he is "in Christ"; he shares Christ's same Spirit with him. This new life in Christ is not merely a matter of coming to a fresh under-standing with one another; it is based on a new creation (Gal. 6:15; 2 Cor. 5:17); it means sharing a new being. The new life which baptism gives does not destroy the old relationships, pro-vided that they can be adapted to the new relationships which now arise; Christianity perfects what is capable of being per-fected. A Christian must be prepared to acknowledge God's achievements in Christ; he must be determined not to overlook God's new creation. Then he will have no difficulty in recog-nizing his brother. Only faith can enable us to appreciate a Christian fully; a Christian must be regarded and loved in faith —despite all the shortcomings the "flesh" is heir to.

My Other Self (vv. 17–20)

The final strophe which rounds off this section of the letter is constructed according to a different pattern (a-b-c-b-a). Onesimus is St. Paul's other self and his heart (a). He will make good any loss the fugitive slave has occasioned his master (b); the debt he incurs in this way is compensated by the debt which Philemon owes him (c). In his approach to Philemon, St. Paul appeals, not to his apostolic authority, but to his union with him through their common sharing in Christ. The final strophe sums up all that is said in the other two double strophes.

[17]If you regard me as a partner [companion], welcome him as myself; [18]if he has done you harm or owes you anything, put it down to my account. [19]I, Paul, write in my own hand: I will make the damage good; not to mention that you, too, owe me your whole self. [20]Yes, brother, I am anxious to make full use of you for once, in the Lord. Refresh my heart in Christ.

Philemon has St. Paul as his partner (companion). One of the effects of being in Christ is that all those who are baptized enjoy fellowship with one another in this new life in Christ. They are all united with Christ and with one another on the level of being. Their life together in society must be viewed and lived in the light of this basic communion which exists between them.

St. Paul refers to Onesimus as his other self: " welcome him as myself." In the new existence which is a fruit of baptism Christ lives in those who are baptized. " It is no longer I who live; Christ lives in me " (Gal. 2:20). St. Paul has a share in Christ and so have Philemon and Onesimus. In a Christian, Christ must be even more apparent than the Christian himself in his ordinary daily life. To see Christ in everyone . . .

Philemon esteemed Paul; if he found it difficult to give his runaway slave a loving welcome, then he should see Paul in him. All the baptized have a share in Christ; they are all other selves to one another. The joy or sorrow one causes another, the love or displeasure he shows affect everyone else who shares the life of the Church. " If one limb is suffering, all the limbs suffer.

If one member is honored, all the others are glad . . ." (1 Cor. 12:26).

Christians are fellow partners; they are brothers of one another. In profane speech, business partners, friends, and married persons are all " sharers," while " brothers " are sons of the same parents; the love such people feel for one another can be expressed in the words, " You are mine and I am yours." In religious language, " sharers " are those who participate in the same meal, at the same table with the divinity in the liturgical assembly (1 Cor. 10:16). The fellow members of religious associations called themselves brothers. According to the language of contemporary (Hellenistic) mysticism, God and man are one. According to St. Paul's mysticism, a Christian shares in Christ; Christians are united in the fellowship of the Son (1 Cor. 1:9). Fellowship with Christ leads to fellowship with all Christians; it involves a fellowship of give and take in all that Christ and Christians enjoy (v. 6). St. Paul can say that it is not he who is alive any more, it is Christ that lives in him (Gal. 2:20), without in any way prejudicing Christ's individual personality or that of Christians. St. Paul's mysticism, which is centered on Christ, involves renouncing oneself for the sake of another. " Welcome him as myself." Such mysticism proves its power by its selfless love of the other.

Communion with Christ is practiced and experienced in the liturgical assembly. The " Supper of the Lord " unites those who partake of it not only with Christ (1 Cor. 11:20), but with one another (1 Cor. 10:17). The many become one body, which is Christ. Their union is symbolized by the fact that they all eat of the same bread and by the plentiful meal to which all contribute and which all share (1 Cor. 11:20ff. and 30). It is clear also from the way they address one another and treat one another as brothers and from the kiss of peace by which they express their mutual harmony (1 Cor. 16:20; 1 Pet. 5:14). Behind all these signs of union and sharing in everything stands the new life in the Spirit which they enjoy.

When Onesimus arrived at Colossae, he came as a member of the household church in Philemon's home. As a baptized Christian, he had the right to participate in the liturgical assembly. He has a right to sit at the same table and be greeted as a brother with the kiss of peace. He is all this because he is now in Christ.

And he is all this for Philemon too. What will Philemon's decision be when the letter which accompanies his slave is read out and discussed in the liturgical assembly? Will he create a chasm between religion and life, he whom St. Paul praises for his faith and love? Welcoming a person, or receiving him back into communion of worship creates an obligation for everyone in the community to treat him as one who has a right to share all they have, as a brother and as another self, in practice as well as in theory.

According to the law of the time, Onesimus had wronged his master by his flight, because of the loss of income he caused him, which was equivalent to stealing—as St. Paul was well aware. This loss had to be made good. Reception into the Church and new life in Christ do not cancel debts incurred during a person's previous life. St. Paul himself is willing to make good the loss Onesimus was responsible for, and he includes a promissory note in his letter. His use of the legal formula, I will make it good, and his signature are meant to give it binding force in law. St. Paul substitutes for Onesimus who is his child, his brother, and his other self. Real love proves itself by deeds; it is ready to stand up for others and take their place even to the point of giving its life on their behalf. This was the way Christ incorporated " the many " into God's kingdom.

With a subtle change of expression—we can almost see his sly laugh—St. Paul quickly draws up an account for Philemon, which concerns him personally. The free man Philemon is a slave in Paul's debt! St. Paul's delightful humor, the " seasoning of speech " (Col. 4:6), and his wit show that a way will be found to receive Onesimus into the community.

Those who have been instrumental in bringing the blessings of redemption to others have a claim to recompense in earthly goods. The Christians at Corinth are indebted to the Christians at Jerusalem because they received the saving gift of faith from them. Therefore, they are bound to pay their debt to the Christians of the first community at Jerusalem by sending them temporal goods (Rom. 15:27). The apostles bestow spiritual blessings as a gift and they have a right, in their turn, to receive the necessaries of life from the faithful (1 Cor. 9:11; Mt. 10:10). It is this mutual give and take which is the foundation of a community.

Philemon owes St. Paul a debt already, himself. The spiritual blessings of the gospel can never be compensated by material benefits. They far surpass all the goods of this world (Mt. 16:26). What can outweigh the gift of eternal life?

Both have a claim by right; St. Paul owes Philemon a debt and Philemon owes Paul. St. Paul's claim is greater and he proposes a compromise. Onesimus (Useful) is useful to Philemon, and by his means St. Paul too is anxious to derive some utility from Philemon. However, the service he seeks is not an earthly one, it is a service in the Lord. He seeks comfort for his anxious heart, peace and joy in the consciousness that the Church is being built up in love (v. 7). Building up the Church with spiritual blessings outweighs all conceivable earthly or material advantages.

Philemon will bring comfort to St. Paul's heart by comforting Onesimus who is his heart. What gives joy to one member of Christ's body gives joy also to others. Seeing the Church being built up brings comfort to all the members of Christ's body.

St. Paul is a father, brother, and another self to the converted slave; he welcomes him as his child, his brother, his other self. These three words express the deepest possible relationships between one person and another; the relationship of father to son, of brother to brother, or a person to his other self. These three relationships touch the chords of a person's heart. Love for another—even if he is beyond the pale—evokes all the resonances of the soul and all its harmonies—love of self, the love of a brother, and the love of a father who is conscious of his responsibility. St. Paul's rule in his pastoral labors as the apostle of the gentiles is summoned up in the phrase, " Becoming all things to all men, to bring everybody salvation " (1 Cor. 9:22).

PERSONAL MESSAGES:
BUILDING UP THE COMMUNITY (vv. 21–24)

St. Paul's concluding sentences recall his opening words once more. The faith and love which prompted him to offer thanks at the beginning of the letter now make him confident that Philemon will do what is best for his slave (v. 21).

In a personal message, St. Paul expresses the hope that he will soon be set free, so that he can come to Colossae (v. 22). In a list of greetings, St. Paul's fellow laborers and the servants of the imprisoned gospel are introduced as intercessors for Onesimus with his master, on his return (23–24). He will not be able to evade them.

Faith and Love (v. 21)

St. Paul realizes that he is asking a lot of Philemon. He excuses himself for being so bold, but he feels entitled to demand a lot because he knows Philemon's faith and love (v. 5).

21I am writing to you, relying on your obedience, knowing that you will do even more than I ask.

St. Paul relies on Philemon's obedience. Faith is obedience. A person who has faith is ready to listen and obey; an exhortation addressed to such a person by way of a request, or a request made by way of exhortation will not fall on deaf ears. A person who is ready to believe is open to love. A person who has ears to hear is prepared to welcome every appeal made to him.

Christians who are obedient make it easy for the Church to welcome a new member.

Philemon's love will go beyond the wish St. Paul expresses in his exhortation. Love is always prepared to do " more " (1 Cor. 13:4). When could love say, That is enough? Generosity opens all doors.

What does St. Paul expect? That Philemon will free his slave? In an earlier letter, he had suggested to the faithful that everyone should continue in his own vocation (1 Cor. 7:20f.). Most likely, he does not want to make any definite suggestion. Love will decide what should be done (2 Cor. 8:8). As love grows, a person's conscience becomes increasingly sensitive to the demands of God's will and the needs of one's fellow men. In this way, it becomes capable of seeing what should be done, what God's will prescribes here and now (Phil. 1:9f.).

St. Paul treats Philemon as an " adult Christian." The decision can be left to him because he has love and practices obedience. These two virtues form the basis of genuine maturity, such as is anxious to promote the welfare of the Church in every way possible.

God's Goodness (v. 22)

Surprisingly, St. Paul now makes arrangements to lodge with Philemon. He has a firm hope that through God's goodness his term of imprisonment will soon be ended. Once more, he must plan for the future.

²²*At the same time [I say], prepare a place for me to stay, because I hope to be reunited with you through your prayers.*

Although he is in prison, St. Paul hopes to visit the community. In his goodness, God will do him this favor. Through the prayers of the faithful, Paul will once again be restored to the community as a favor, just as the converted slave is also being returned to them as a favor.

Philemon has already been praised for his faith (v. 5). His active faith, which proves itself by love, will also be manifested in his hospitality. He will give St. Paul a warm welcome, just as he learned from the beginning of his Christian life to welcome the gift of faith which came to him through the message St. Paul preached. Sacred scripture uses the same word for the welcome given to a guest as for the welcome given to God's word (Lk. 8:13; Acts 8:14).

Prepare a place for me to stay, is the only command St. Paul gives in the whole letter. But this command is in answer to an invitation made long before. St. Paul commands where we should expect him to make a request and he makes a request where we should expect him to command. He has no wish to domineer over a Christian whose life is founded on faith; rather he wants to help him to achieve happiness as his fellow laborer (2 Cor. 1:24). The Church is built up by readiness to serve, not by anxiety to domineer.

Servants of the Gospel (vv. 23–24)

The list of greetings contains the same names as Colossians 4:10–14. Epaphras heads the list; he had founded the churches at Colossae, Hierapolis, and Laodicea (Col. 4:13). Because of the ministry he exercised, he shares Paul's imprisonment. Mark had been a companion of St. Paul at one stage, but then he abandoned him; now he is with him once more. Aristarchus from Thessalonica had shared all his sufferings faithfully (Acts 19:29; 27:2). Demas later left St. Paul out of love for this present world (2 Tim. 4:10). Luke, the beloved physician (Col. 4:14), is the author of the third gospel and a disciple of St. Paul.

23Epaphras sends his greetings, my fellow prisoner in Christ Jesus, 24[and] Mark, Aristarchus, Demas, Luke, my co-workers.

St. Paul wrote his letter as a martyr and an apostle. He includes greetings from his fellow prisoner in Christ Jesus and those who shared his labors, his fellow martyrs and his fellow apostles. The Church is built up by apostles and martyrs; this involves hard work and a constant battle (Epaphras is a fellow prisoner of war). It takes Jesus' message and his blood to incorporate a new member into the Church.

As they send their greetings, the apostles and martyrs implore the community to give a loving welcome to the brother who is to be incorporated into the Church, even if this means overcoming their own self-love and subduing it.

THE CLOSE OF THE LETTER
(v. 25)

CONCLUSION (v. 25)

The letter begins and ends with a blessing such as was used in the liturgy.

[25]*The grace of the Lord Jesus Christ be with your spirit. Amen.*

The grace (*charis*) which our Lord Jesus Christ possesses and which he dispenses must fill the community in Philemon's house to the depths of their hearts and inspire all their decisions. *Charis* (grace, charm) characterizes the whole letter and it must be effective in its recipients too. It must constitute the spiritual atmosphere which awaits Onesimus on his return.

The letter ends with a short formula of blessing and greeting. In his other letters, St. Paul uses a more elaborate formula, as in the blessing which closes the Second Epistle to the Corinthians, "The grace of our Lord Jesus Christ, and the love of God, and the imparting of the Holy Spirit be with you all. Amen" (13:13). Father, Son, and Holy Spirit are all mentioned in this formula and particular gifts are attributed to each one. However, all three mean the same spiritual gift which St. Paul here mentions by way of summing up everything—the grace of the Lord Jesus Christ. This is the gift of love which comes from the heart of the triune God. It overflows upon the faithful, so that all their thoughts and actions may be performed in a way which is worthy of God. This will strengthen their active love of their brothers and inflame them with new love for God.

In the liturgy, the prayer of blessing is followed by an *Amen*

99

pronounced by the congregation. In this way, the community will also say Amen to this letter, when it is read out in the liturgical assembly. In union with St. Paul, they will pray for the grace which comes to us as a gift from above and creates the "atmosphere" in which all feel free to approach one another in love.